# The Road to 2084

Val Bakh

# CONTENTS

# AUTHOR'S FOREWORD

There are way too many political, economic, and social theories about the contraposition of Left versus Right, each claiming itself to be the ultimate truth. Picking the right theory that would explain it all is as impossible as choosing the right model of a car on your first try. This book is my modest attempt to bring some clarity regarding the central political conflict of all times. I admit I am not a political scientist, economist, psychologist, or sociologist. Then what on Earth makes me believe that *my* theory is The One?

Well, I am not trying to pretend I have discovered something that no one else had thought of. Most of what this book is about is based on the philosophy of historical materialism. However, I am not a Marxist; in fact, I am anything but. I just happen to agree with the foundational principle of the Marxist theory that physical reality is primary and our consciousness is secondary, that's all. I believe that Marxism more or less correctly explains the early stages of our history but loses traction somewhere in the middle of the capitalist stage and goes completely off course when it comes to socialism and communism.

I am one of those people who spent a significant chunk of their life on the other side of the Iron Curtain, where studying various aspects of Marxism-Leninism was mandatory. So, unlike a vast majority of the so-called Free World that knows very little or nothing at all about Marxism, I have the advantage of being able to compare the two sides. As you probably know, the devil is usually in the details, and I've lived through quite a few of those.

So, please keep in mind that this book is NOT a proper scientific research; rather, it is my personal take on what I believe to be the most important issue of our time: *Where are we, as a society, heading?* It is intended as light reading for those who are curious about the true nature of socialism and communism, and also as a primer, of sorts, for newbies to global politics in general. I hope I've been reasonably objective and logical and that I've kept it simple enough for anyone who is interested to understand without falling asleep within the first five or ten minutes of reading.

Val Bakh

# INTRODUCTION

No one can deny that the world we live in has been changing ever since its inception. First humans roamed the Earth stark naked or wrapped in skins of the animals they had hunted down and eaten. Now we live in air-conditioned houses with flush toilets, refrigerators, and Internet access; we drive cars and fly in airplanes; and the only place we hunt for food is the local supermarket. So, are we already at the end of our road, with eternal bliss in sight, or are there more turns for us to go through? Is our destination a good place or not so much so? Is it all somehow predetermined or can we plot our own course? We'll try to provide some insight into these issues for those who are interested in better understanding of the world we live in. Most existing books and articles on societal and historical subjects are eye-glazers for insomniacs and are not exactly healthy for reading by mortal humans. They are primarily intended as a sleeping-pill substitute for those who are allergic to medicine. But if you want it short and sweet and straight to the point—read on; you are in the right place now.

There are many forms of life on our planet, and some of them, reportedly, have even more sophisticated brains than humans do. But for reasons that scientists and theologians are still arguing about, only we, the human species, are in a position to consciously pave our own way. We have the ability to think abstractly and apply logic. Given the same set of initial conditions, logic—by its very nature—is supposed to lead everyone to the same conclusions. However, despite all of us living on the same planet, different people, even next-door neighbours and members of the same family, more often than not disagree on the best socio-economic order and the best way to attain it.

With the innumerable varieties of flavours in modern-day politics, coming up with a single universally accepted classification is virtually impossible. So, any attempt to define who stands for what should be regarded with a grain of salt. But despite all the difficulties of this task, it's reasonably safe to say that the political spectrum, in essence, boils down to the Left and the Right. The terms have nothing to do with being right or wrong. Historically, they originate from the way members of the National Assembly in France used to choose their seats back in 1789.

Among all the existing theories of human history, one has had—and is still having—an enormous impact on the society. Karl Marx and Friedrich Engels, two German political scientists of the 19th century, came up with a philosophy of historical materialism, which essentially is the theoretical foundation for communism. Half a century later, one of their most devout followers Vladimir Ulyanov, aka Lenin, practically applied the Marxist theory to Russia. In 1917, the Russian Communists led by Lenin seized power in Russia and embarked on a 75-year-long unprecedented socio-economic experiment. The ensuing confrontation between the Soviet Union—the name the Russian Communists used for their newly conquered empire—and the rest of the so-called civilized world was the major political factor that had shaped most of the 20th century.

Marxism and its various revisions form the left end of the political spectrum. By implication, those who oppose Marxism are deemed to live on the right side. Generally speaking, the stronger their opposition is, the farther to the right they live. Because over the last 20 years or so we have been witnessing a very strong rise of the Left all over the world, especially among young people, it is becoming increasingly important to clearly understand where this trend may be leading us. What if we end up in a place that is anything *but* sunshine and lollypops? When you find yourself in a moving vehicle, knowing its exact destination almost always seems like a good idea, regardless of anyone's political inclinations or affiliations.

# Chapter 1
# MARXISM 101

Accrding to the Marxist theory, human societies pass in their development through six stages, or phases: primaeval communities, slavery, feudalism, capitalism, socialism, and communism. The theory refers to those stages as socio-economic formations. Each formation is defined by its two components: an economic basis, or foundation, and a social superstructure. The type of economic basis is reflective of who owns means of production, and it predetermines the type of superstructure, which encompasses the social relationships that govern a given society at the time. While the type of superstructure corresponds to the type of basis, the society is developing in relative harmony. Occasionally, the existing social relationships start hindering further economic growth. At those critical points, the superstructure has to change in order to adapt to a new type of economic basis. Some transformations occur peacefully and stretch over decades, whereas some take the form of violent and relatively quick revolutions.

The theory claims that generally a society *must* go through this succession of phases until it reaches the last one—communism, which is, supposedly, the ultimate goal and the bright future of humankind. In some specific cases, a society might skip a phase or two and jump, for example, from feudalism directly to socialism. The phases are merely theoretical concepts and may not actually exist in their pure forms. In real life, there is often a mingle of economic and social relationships, especially during transitions from one phase to the next. Some combinations do not easily fit into the main theory. For example, the United States of America went through a bizarre mix of slavery and capitalism. Because these two formations are not adjacent in the succession line, the fathers of Marxism—Karl Marx and Friedrich Engels—had to go an extra mile to theoretically explain the phenomenon. According to them, slavery can take a variety of forms, ranging from explicit ownership of humans by other humans to more subtle dependencies of wage-earners upon their employers. Thus broadly defined, slavery becomes an inherent element of any society that is based on exploitation and is therefore easier to explain when it suddenly pops up at a place

4

where it normally doesn't belong. And it also fits nicely into the main theory, whose primary goal is to convince us that capitalism is *bad*. How could it be good if it's nothing but a slightly disguised form of slavery?

Marxism contends that each next formation is better than its predecessor in the sense that it expands personal freedoms of individual members of a society and is yet another step on the road to universal equality. The fact that communism is supposed to be the ultimate goal defines which direction is deemed forward. By implication, any movement towards communism is advancement, or *progress*. Thus *progressives*, by definition, are those people who strive for communism. This is true regardless of whether those people approve of communism or whether they even realize what the definition really means. Those progressives who realize and approve don't shy away from the label; on the contrary, they stick it on their foreheads and wear it with pride and defiance. Those who don't approve of communism and don't realize where the definition of the term *progressive* is coming from would usually, when confronted, try to obfuscate the issue by providing alternative definitions that would paint progressives as harmless soft-hearted liberals somewhere just a tick to the left of the Centre. But that is a different part of the story, and we'll cover it a bit later.

Back to our 101 crash course, let's now take a quick look at each socio-economic formation.

## Primaeval Communities

In primaeval communities, any social structures were rudimentary or non-existent and people were associated through their respective tribal and family lines. Economically, all that the people did was simply provide sustenance for themselves by living off what Nature had to offer. When natural resources became scarce in one place, its inhabitants moved to another, and stronger tribes tried to conquer and enslave their neighbours and seize their territories. This expansion denotes the beginnings of the slavery formation.

## Slavery

In the classic, ancient-times slavery, there were two major groups of people, or classes: slaves and masters. Slaves were their masters' property and in practical terms had no rights or personal freedoms whatsoever. They had to work for their masters for free, could not leave without their masters' permission, were traded as a commodity, and passed on their enslavement to their descendants. Slaves lived exclusively off their masters' handouts. Not all of the so-called free people (i.e., those who were not slaves) were masters; some were poorer than others, and many did not have any slaves at all. Although the immediate goals and needs of the rich and of the poor are typically different, the main economic objectives in those times still, ultimately, revolved around necessities of life—mostly food and clothing—which came primarily from agriculture. Slavery did not provide any incentives for the enslaved beyond their mere physical survival. Eventually, a certain limit was reached when slave labour alone could no longer produce enough food and clothing for everyone. Most of the known world had already been conquered, which put a natural limit on the expansion of slavery.

## Feudalism

At that point in human history, feudal relationships started forming. Slaves and masters were gradually replaced with landlords and serfs. Landlords leased plots of their land to serfs; serfs worked on those lands for their own profit and paid rent. The payments could come in the form of money or as a portion of one's harvest or labour. Unlike slaves, serfs were technically free; they had some—minimal—rights and personal freedoms. In reality, they were attached to their allocated plots of land and passed their serfdom to their children. And again, as not everyone was necessarily either a slave or a master in the slavery phase, there were significant numbers of people during feudalism who were neither serfs nor landlords. Those were free farmers, in the countryside, and trade or commerce professionals, in cities. They were the beginnings of the bourgeoisie. As human economic activities started expanding beyond purely agricultural production, serfdom eventually died off. Industrial production required a mobile, unattached work force rather than stationary serfs stuck on their lands.

## Capitalism

Capitalism is probably the most interesting formation, primarily because it is the phase we are still living in now. There are so many flavours to it that sometimes it's not easy to even recognize it for what it really is, let alone trying to come up with a meaningful classification of the entire motley assortment that is presently in existence. For our 101 level, it should suffice to focus on the classic capitalist model. All the other models differ from it by only a degree and nature of government intervention.

The two cornerstones of classic capitalism are private property and profit. The former refers to means of production being in private ownership, and the latter refers to profit being the goal of any business activity. Capitalists are those individuals who own businesses. They hire workers and pay them money for producing goods or services. Marxism deems this type of relationship exploitation of a person by a person: capitalists exploit workers. A capitalist arrogates the products of workers' labour on the grounds that the capitalist owns the means of production that were used to produce the goods or services. The workers have no rights on the products of their labour; the workers' only function in this relationship is to sell their skills and efforts for money. The capitalist sells the produced goods or services on the open market and makes profit from the difference between the going sales prices, on one hand, and the workers' salaries, operating expenses, and the cost of any raw materials, on the other hand.

If workers are paid for their work, then why is it exploitation? In terms of economics, exploitation means inadequately compensating someone's labour, or underpaying a worker. Marxism contends that the only way capitalists can make profit is by paying workers less than their work is actually worth, that is, by paying them properly for only part of their work and leaving the rest of their work unpaid, thereby robbing the workers. This view makes the working class, or proletariat, the oppressed and makes capitalists the oppressors. Workers are the ones who actually *make* things, and capitalists are useless parasites living off their workers' labour. Consequently, the elimination of capitalists as a class would do nothing but good; it would liberate workers and would not adversely affect any processes whereby goods or services are being produced. Obviously, there is a whole lot more to both capitalism and the Marxist take on it, but to keep things simple here, we'll leave our analyses for later.

## Socialism

Socialism also comes in a plenty of shapes and forms, ranging from Orwellian-style totalitarian prison camps to incarnations so mild that even political scientists have a hard time telling them apart from certain flavours of capitalism. The Marxist theory defines socialism based on the same two fundamental criteria that it uses to define capitalism: the type of property and the economic goal. Socialism features (a) state or collective ownership of means of production and (b) direct usefulness of produced goods, or use-value, in Marxist terminology. Thus under socialism, all means of production are owned by the people, and the main goal of any business is to produce goods or services that satisfy certain needs of the people. Being profitable no longer matters to a business, as long as it produces something that people need or want.

Since all means of production belong to the people, any profit or loss is shared among all society's members. Although money still exists, its role is reduced to being merely the means of account in relation to remuneration for work and to sales of consumer goods and services. Those who work more or whose work is more important for the society are paid more money and thus can purchase more consumer goods and services. The entire economy is planned by the government, based on the needs of the people. Provided the planning is done properly and everything works as planned, the economy can develop smoothly, without the cycles of growth and recession characteristic of capitalism. Consequently, claims the Marxist theory, socialism can outperform capitalism and satisfy people's needs in a more meaningful way.

## Communism

Marxism deems socialism an intermediate, transitional phase from capitalism to communism. The latter requires abundance of consumer goods and services, so that their distribution can be based on one's needs and wants rather than on his or her contribution to their production. The theory assumes that everyone who can work will be conscientious enough to work voluntarily. Essentially, communism is viewed as an ideal socio-economic arrangement, the ultimate destination on the road to universal prosperity and happiness. Once all countries on Earth have reached this phase, there will be no need for governments or even countries. Everyone will be completely free of any kind of oppression or exploitation. That is supposed to be the crowning achievement for the human species, the land of universal and never-ending milk-and-honey or sunshine-and-lollypops, depending on your dietary preference.

## Chapter 2
# CAPITALISM VS. SOCIALISM

Capitalism and socialism are the two most relevant phases for us. Capitalism is our present, and socialism—the past experiments notwithstanding—is where the Left are trying to push or, in some cases, drag, us. Let's put them side-by-side and do some comparisons.

### Profit

Under capitalism, the main objective and driving force of virtually any business is profit. A capitalist invests money to build a factory, company, firm—the exact type of business entity or nature of the business activity are unimportant—hires personnel to do the necessary work, and collects revenues from sales of the produced physical merchandise or rendered services.

Marxism claims that the capitalist robs workers by paying them for less work than they actually perform and that this unpaid difference is what makes profit possible. Provided the product sells for a high enough price and in sufficient quantity, the capitalist, indeed, can collect more revenue than the total of all relevant expenses, including workers' salaries. In that case, revenue minus expenses equals profit. If extracting profit is robbery and if *this* is the amount workers have been allegedly deprived of, then it logically follows that to stop being a bad guy the capitalist should increase the workers' pay so as to make zero profit. Then why would the capitalist start the business in the first place? He has invested his own money to set everything up, whereas workers came to him with nothing but their skills and sometimes without even that. True, some of the workers may have invested *their* money in learning the necessary skills, so that they could sell those skills on the labour market. That's what they have voluntarily chosen to invest in: not in building their own businesses and becoming capitalists but in acquiring skills in order to become workers.

For those who are paying attention to political correctness (sometimes also known as PC BS), the capitalist here is a "he" only as a manner of speech, for brevity; in reality, it can also be a "she" or "they." This also applies to workers, politicians, and whoever else we might mention later on.

Both sides—a capitalist and his employees—are taking risks, but they are very different types of risks. Revenue minus expenses is not guaranteed to always be a positive value. If the result is negative, then what the capitalist gets is no longer a profit; it is called a loss. Does this mean the capitalist has overpaid his workers? Does being a good guy mean sharing with his workers only his profits or does it also include sharing his losses? If the capitalist suffers a loss, he has only two options: either to cover the loss from his own pocket and keep going or to get rid of the business altogether—sell it or close down. Either way, the capitalist would typically lose a very significant amount of his own money, and the probability of this happening is not negligible. On the other hand, when a worker invests in acquiring education or professional skills, his chances of not being able to subsequently find a job are pretty slim. Of course, finding a job is not exactly easy, especially during a recession. But if those seeking employment keep trying, sooner or later they will almost always eventually succeed. Hence their investments in education or training are almost never lost. Whereas if a business goes under, it's gone; the unsuccessful capitalist who has lost his assets has no choice but to become a worker for a more successful capitalist. This is all, of course, oversimplification—just to illustrate the point. Real life is a lot more complex. However, the main principle still stands: A capitalist risks his very own money, and a worker's only risk is that he might need to find another job.

## Initial Capital Accumulation

Is the choice between becoming a worker and becoming a capitalist just a matter of personal preference? Can *anyone* become one or the other by simply making a conscious decision, without regard to any other, external factors? Where is the money for an initial investment supposed to come from? Clearly, *nothing* can beget nothing but *nothing*; everything must always start with *something*. You can't just wake up one day, decide that becoming a millionaire seems like a good idea, go to a department store, and buy yourself a few of those millions. To buy something—anything—you need money. Hence you must have worked somewhere before and have earned and saved enough for your purchase. That's what Adam Smith, a Scottish philosopher and political economist of the 18$^{th}$ century, suggested in the 1770s.

About a hundred years later, Karl Marx had an entirely different idea. According to him, you must have robbed someone on your way to the store. Right from the very beginning, Marxism rejects the idea that initial capital could have been acquired legitimately. So, does this mean that, one way or another, all capitalists started as bad guys and all workers are, by definition, victims? If you've got a business, you didn't build that? Someone else did it for you, and you just stole it from him? Adam Smith says those who were smarter or who worked harder, over time, accumulated wealth sufficient to start a business, and those who were less industrious or less frugal did not. As a result, the latter had no choice but to go work for the former in order to provide for themselves. Karl Marx contends this is nothing else but a joke similar to original sin: Adam—not Smith, of course; *this* Adam is the proverbial guy from the Bible—bites an apple, and all humans automatically become sinners. Marx says the original accumulation of capital almost certainly must have involved sin: it could have occurred through resource extraction (i.e., plunder of Nature) or through conquest and ensuing direct plunder and possibly enslavement of the conquered. Hence the notorious "apology tours" of certain Left-minded politicians, global wealth redistribution scams like Global Warming (recently renamed Climate Change), as well as the never-ending stream of direct aid to Third World countries.

There are lots of smart and hard-working people, say Marxists. Why are not all of them capitalists? According to Adam Smith, they are either not smart enough or not hard-working enough or simply prefer not to bother. According to Karl Marx, they or their ancestors must have been ripped off by some evil folks, who then used the booty to start businesses and to force those smart hard-working people into wage-enslavement.

Which of these two opposing points of view is the right one? Real life is never clear-cut black-and-white; there are always shades of grey in-between and a whole universe of other colours as well. Some capitalists or their ancestors may have, indeed, acquired their wealth while wearing black hats. At the same time, there are quite a few of those who started in a teeny-weenie office or workshop in their parents' basement or garage and then went global through hard work and perseverance. Realistically, becoming a capitalist or a worker may not always be just a matter or unconstrained choice and personal preference. But nor is it always a destiny. Sometimes someone who never even dreamed of becoming a capitalist gets lucky, and sometimes someone who has been dreaming of nothing else but— never gets a chance to start his own business. The bottom line is: *it is what it is*. Some people are good guys, some are bad ones, and both kinds can be found everywhere. Some capitalists may wear black hats, and some workers may proudly flaunt white ones. And it is equally true that some capitalists are decent folks and some workers are scoundrels.

## Use-Value

The primary objective of any capitalist, assert Marxists, is profit. Their very definition of capital is *money that is used to make more money*. Capitalists don't care what to produce, as long as they can make profit off it. It is unwise, claim Marxists, for a society to start producing things just to find out that no one needs or wants them. It is wasteful for multiple companies to manufacture the same goods and compete for the same consumers when just one or two of those companies could satisfy the existing demand. Also, profit is a bad thing because it is made through exploitation. Let's eliminate profit as the driving force of the economy and build a better, fairer society, they say, where the primary goal of any business will only be to produce something that people need. Private property will then have to go because no one sane would want to risk their personal fortunes to run businesses without making profit. The entire society—through its government—should own all means of production.

Usually, the word *expropriation* refers to a situation where a government takes away someone's property—with or without compensation, depending on the specific circumstances—for the good of the general public. In Marxist terminology, expropriation has a wider meaning; it covers a multitude of scenarios where various types of entities forcibly take away private property from other entities. According to Marxism, all initial capital was accumulated through one form of expropriation or another. All capitalist production is also nothing else but a slightly disguised form of expropriation—the source of profit is an unpaid portion of a worker's labour, remember? Essentially, it's like theft or robbery. So, it is only fair for workers to expropriate the expropriators—in other words, to take away all privately owned means of production without any compensation. After all, capitalists are parasites; they don't perform any useful function. All they do is get rich on the backs of the working people. Removing capitalists from the equation will have no effect on the actual, physical production, because capitalists don't work.

It's really hard to tell now where this idea came from. How many business owners do you know who don't personally manage what they own? Who would *completely* trust others to do it for them? Under the classic-capitalism model, even if a company is run on a day-to-day basis by a hired professional manager, the owner would usually still be personally involved in high-level oversight and strategic decision-making. In the contemporary economic reality, most shareholders of publicly-traded companies are, indeed, typically, detached from the management process. However, strictly speaking, those people are not true capitalists, because ownership of such companies is, in essence, public; that's why they are called publicly-traded.

Maybe Marx felt that being part of management didn't count as work because, in the 19th century, workers' labour was significantly more physical? This is merely a speculation, but it seems like a good guess. In the former Soviet Union, whose official ideology was based on Marxism, a pervasive perception carefully cultivated by the authorities was that, to count as *real* work, it had to necessarily involve getting one's hands dirty.

Anyway, according to the theory, socialism is based on social ownership of means of production. What is social ownership? Marxism defines it as ownership either by the entire society—technically, via the government—or by groups of workers. The latter is known as co-operative type of ownership: a group of workers collectively own a company for which they work. We'll take a closer look at co-operatives under socialism a bit later. For now it is safe to disregard them because they don't make any noticeable difference under the mainstream, classic socialist model. Or to be more accurate, socialism can survive in its classic form for only as long as it keeps co-operatives on a tight leash.

Since profit no longer matters, workers themselves—through the government, which under socialism supposedly represents all the working people—decide what, where, how, and how much to produce, depending on what people need. The primary objective of production now is use-value, a concept that represents an actual need for a product. Quantitatively, use-value of a specific product is expressed in units of measure appropriate for that product. For example, the use-value of a tonne of grain is one tonne. As profit is no longer a consideration, the role of money in a socialist economy is significantly different than that in a capitalist economy.

Because a socialist enterprise is not required to make profit, it doesn't matter for it how much it will pay for any materials, equipment, or services that it needs to purchase from other companies and how much it will be paid for what it produces. Consequently, exchange of non-consumer goods and services between businesses does not have to be expressed in monetary terms. Even if it is, then it's only for convenience of accounting rather than out of necessity. The only time that money matters is when you go to a store to buy consumer goods. In theory, *that* money is supposed to represent your contribution to the welfare of your country. Everyone under socialism is supposed to be equal, but as Lenin used to point out, complete equality can exist only in a cemetery. In fact, this idea comes from a German proverb, but Lenin, reportedly, did like to mention it, on occasion. So, some people end up being more equal than others. They deserve more pleasures of life, which requires more money. Someone high up the food chain scratches his head, pokes his nose, or contemplates a scenic view out of his office window and thus decides how much mortal humans should be paid for their efforts and how much stuff they should be able to purchase with that money. Essentially, the government can print any amount of cash it sees fit. The only purpose of that cash is to be paid out in workers' salaries. The real value of such money depends on the prices of the available consumer goods and services. This cash cannot be used to pay for industrial goods or services in business-to-business relationships. The latter use a completely unrelated type of money, which in the Soviet Union was commonly referred to as *non-cash*. Later, we'll see how well this dual-money arrangement actually worked.

Well, there is one other scenario where money under socialism matters. In its trade relationships with capitalist countries, the Soviet Union had to use real money—either foreign currencies or commonly accepted valuables, such as gold or diamonds. But those dealings were not an inherent part of the classic socialist economic model. All contacts with the outside world were strictly controlled by the central government. Individual enterprises had neither the authority nor financial means of their own to enter into any international agreements without the government's sponsorship. In relationships with friendly socialist countries, the Soviet Union used a special, "international" version of non-cash.

Back to use-value vs. profit now. Which criterion works better? On the surface, use-value makes a lot more sense. Theoretically, people elect their government, and the government decides what to produce to better satisfy people's needs. No unnecessary duplication of effort, no wasteful overproduction, no brazen excessive consumption by few haves while the majority of have-nots make do with scraps. In reality, however, humans are prone to making mistakes. Even though the Communist Party is divinely infallible, its high priests who decide how much bread and butter should suffice to feed regular mortals are—surprise?—humans. When cost is not a directly constraining factor, nothing can prevent an ambitious bureaucrat from launching an ambitious project without much regard to the realities of life.

An example of such blatant idiocy is the decision by Nikita Khrushchev, the Soviet leader from 1953 till 1964, to significantly increase cultivation of corn, which came at the expense of traditional Russian cereals: wheat and rye. The idea was that corn would provide a lot more cattle feed and thus help produce more meat and dairy products. Unfortunately, not being a member of the Communist Party, politically irresponsible corn failed to fully cooperate; it freakishly required various chemicals and a warm climate, neither of which were in abundance in the Soviet Union. Combined with a couple of similar moronic projects successfully bungled by the wise Soviet leadership at the time, the end result was bread rationing in the early 1960s and severe shortages of meat and butter for decades to come. To alleviate the bread problem, Khrushchev spent tons of gold and pretty much exhausted the country's foreign currency reserves to buy grain from black-hat imperialists in the West. Unable to increase production of foodstuffs, the Soviet leadership found it more expedient to meet the demand by … reducing it. In 1962 they jacked up prices for meat and butter and, while they were at it, raised workers' output norms too (We'll just have to work harder …). A protest in the city of Novocherkassk was drowned in blood—lest other irresponsible elements were tempted to make any more waves. Eventually, two years later, Nikita Khrushchev was deposed from his throne, but the System remained, and the new leadership was free to make its own fair share of scot-free mistakes. Examples are plenty; almost the entire history of the Soviet Union and its former socialist allies is full of them.

No one is perfect; anyone can make a mistake. When we make one, shouldn't we try to correct it as soon as it is discovered and then learn from the experience? Unfortunately, it's not as easy as it might sound. Under socialism, only the gravest blunders can cause direct and obvious effects like famine or massive social unrest. With their unrestricted power, communist regimes can afford to turn a blind eye to the former and drown in blood the latter. But more commonly, without the requirement for each and every undertaking to be profitable, there are usually no immediate and clear signs of trouble when something goes wrong.

For example, some high-positioned decision makers in the Soviet Union came up with an idea of diverting water from a couple of rivers uselessly, in their opinion, dumping cubic kilometres of water into the Aral Sea, formerly the fourth-largest lake on the planet. The water was supposed to irrigate the nearby desert and thereby boost production of cotton, rice, melons, and other useful things. Channels had been dug across the desert and water had been redirected, but then it was discovered that more than half of that water either evaporated on its long way to the crop fields or simply vanished into the sand bed. Digging hundreds of thousands of kilometres of channels in the sand is quite a bit of work in itself. But water-proofing all of that is outright impossible in any reasonable time frame. Even now, over 70 years after the digging started, less than a quarter of the overall canal lengths are equipped with anti-filtration linings, which, by the way, reduce water loss by mere 15 percent. The most obvious effects of this truly cosmic-scale endeavour—the inevitable destruction of the Aral Sea and the resulting extinction of the surrounding population—took decades to develop. But besides that, there were also significant latent consequences that could not be easily traced to their cause and, as it becomes to socialism, were quietly shared among the entire population—except, of course, members of the Inner Party, who were responsible for those woes and whose wives did their shopping in special stores closed to the general public.

The cost of all the machinery, equipment, and materials was "paid" in non-cash. The word *paid* is enclosed in quotation marks because the costs were not *really* paid, at least, not in the same sense that applies when we take our shopping cart through a check-out counter. Non-cash was a sort of Monopoly money; any quantities of it could be effortlessly conjured at any time out of thin air by a mere authorized bureaucrat's signature. Non-cash existed only in the form of meaningless numbers on state-owned organizations' accounts in state-owned banks. Since the money was not real, neither were any "payments" made in it nor arbitrarily assigned prices. If a company turned any profit, it was automatically devoured by the black hole at the top of the food chain. If a company ended up in the red, any losses were covered by handouts from above. The overall balance was of no consequence, because the hole was black, after all.

The cost of the digging, however, was paid in cash, which did have certain value attached to it. Of course, the Soviet government could print any necessary quantities of coloured pieces of paper with numbers on them. But doing so would not significantly affect the end result, because the value of cash money was determined not by how many pieces of pied paper one had in his pocket but rather by quantity and quality of available consumer goods and services. To pay to the diggers, you can print as much cash as you want, but unless you correspondingly increase production of consumer goods, all you have done is merely dilute all of the cash currently in circulation. A rank-and-file Soviet slogger wouldn't feel an immediate pang of sharp pain each time an additional banknote was printed to pay for an additional kilometre of a canal dug in the sand, but quality of life in the country would inevitably keep sliding down day after day, year after year ... But why would living standards dwindle? If you are capable of digging light-years of canals in a desert, what might possibly prevent you from producing a few more TV sets, refrigerators, or just bottles of vodka? It turns out that you can't always do both at the same time. There were only so many people in the country. The more of them were sent to do the digging, the fewer of them were left to produce personally-consumable use-value to match the volume of printed cash in circulation at the time.

Now let's compare this to capitalism. Its driving force is profit. A symbol of greed?—At the surface, it might appear so; a capitalist, indeed, does not care what to produce, as long as he makes profit. But for the profit to happen, someone must *buy* the product. If there are enough buyers for a price high enough, he wins. If no one wants his product, he's out of business faster than he can say "Oops." Thus profit is not entirely a symbol of greed; it is also an impartial judge and sometimes an unforgiving executioner. By weeding out the unfit and ill-equipped, profit—or, in certain cases, lack thereof—ensures that only the stuff that has proper use-value is produced.

Some critics of capitalism point out that profit being the only goal often causes businesses to aggressively market and make us want things that we don't really need ("Supply creates its own demand"). But isn't it *our* money? Aren't we entitled to the power of our sweat-soaked dollar? No one forces us to buy a third cell-phone or a hundred-and-twentieth pair of shoes. Ultimately, it's our decision. What do we prefer: to personally exercise our unalienable right to be stupid under capitalism or to delegate this right to a government bureaucrat under socialism?

## Capitalist Economic Cycles

Capitalism is haphazard because there is no central planning; every producer is for himself. When something—generally, it can be anything, any type of product—is in high demand, prices for that thing go up. Why?—Because capitalists always want to make more profit, and in a high-demand environment they can.

Let's consider one specific type of consumer goods, such as TV sets, and use it as an example. At first, TVs are so attractive that consumers are willing to buy them, even at a higher price and even at the expense of some other goods they can do without. Higher prices lead to higher profits, which in turn attract more investments in production of the desired thing. The more TVs are produced, the more they become available. Consequently, the less people want to buy them. Why?—Supply has met the demand, and they are now in a balance. To boost sales, manufacturers have to lower prices, thereby attracting additional consumers, those who earlier could not afford the TVs at their peak prices. Lower prices cut into profit, which in turn discourages new investments in producing the same TV sets in the same ways. Instead, those investments will rather finance technological or technical progress: either a capitalist learns how to make those old TVs for a fraction of their original cost (and thus prolong the current cycle), or he comes up with a better TV (and thereby starts a new cycle). That's how colour TVs replaced black-and-whites and how elegant flat-panels killed bulky CRTs and rear-projections. By the way, socialist countries lagged behind in those areas by approximately a decade.

In a consumer-oriented economy, one thing leads to another and, ultimately, leads to a chain reaction. To exploit the TV example a little more, let's say there's an explosive increase in TV sales at a certain point in time. This attracts investments—TV production grows—more jobs are created—more people earn good salaries—more people have more money to spend—demands for other products start growing. Capitalists make more profit—they have more money to invest—they invest in products that satisfy new, growing demands—those investments create new jobs—... The ascending curve continues for a while and then reaches a point where all current demands are adequately satisfied. This doesn't mean that paradise has finally descended to Earth and now everyone has everything that there is to have. The demand is satisfied in a statistical sense: some people might still have almost nothing and some might have two or three of everything. Absolute equality is only in a cemetery, remember? In fact, even *that* is a joke; some tombstones are bigger than others.

Anyway, at that point, prices—and, hence, profits—become so low that capitalists significantly lose their incentive to produce more. On the contrary, many are operating at a loss and, therefore, have to slow down in order to reduce their losses. That launches a chain reaction in the opposite direction. Less production—fewer jobs—less money earned—less money to spend—lower demand—even lower prices—even less production—... The downward spiral continues until the tumbling supply finally overtakes the drying out demand. Once supply has become lower than demand, prices start rising back again.

This model of economic cycles is purely theoretical; it applies only to classic capitalism, which doesn't exist in reality. In real life, there are all sorts of external factors that are superimposed on the economic factors and make it pretty much impossible to identify a single, root cause of any specific crisis, especially taking into account how good politicians on both sides of the aisle have become in successfully obfuscating any issue. Then what's the point of analyzing a theory that doesn't jibe with reality?

The point is that this theory is still the foundation of everything else. All those external factors do not happen of their own volition. No one likes recessions. Workers don't like them because of high unemployment, which leads to decline in living standards. Capitalists don't like them because some lose profits and others lose everything. Therefore, no wonder that everyone is trying to come up with a remedy, something that will either smoothen negative effects of recessions or rid them altogether. Everyone claims that *their* remedy is the panacea. Governments are under pressure from all sides to do *something*. And they, indeed, do; some do one thing, others try another. And that is where the Law of Unintended Consequences kicks in. Trying to fix one thing, a government usually botches another. Unhappy voters get themselves another government, which fixes what the previous government screwed up and in the process ruins something else. After a few election cycles, the situation becomes so entangled that the society loses hope of any government being able to fix anything at all and becomes quite receptive to radical solutions, like cutting the knot altogether, replacing the system that seemingly doesn't work—capitalism—with one that supposedly does—socialism. How well it works and why—we'll discuss in due course. For now let's see if there is anything that *can* work at all.

Suppose you are driving a car and you see a straight and particularly boring stretch of a highway. Naturally, you want to go faster so that you can reach your destination sooner. You floor the gas pedal, and the car starts accelerating. But you can't keep accelerating all the time. First of all, there is a technical limit to how fast your car can go. And secondly, you shouldn't drive at the top speed lest you ruin the engine. So, you accelerate to a certain point, until you feel you are going fast enough, and then you try to maintain that optimal speed for as long as you need. Regardless of whether your car is equipped with cruise control, the process is essentially the same: the speed never stays constant but rather goes slightly up or down, depending on whether it falls short of the chosen level or exceeds it, respectively. It is technically impossible for your car to avoid these cycles; it simply *can't* go at *exactly* the same speed for any significant periods of time. As a driver, you can try to work the gas pedal more smoothly to minimize those deviations; or as a car designer, you can try to improve the cruise control system to do that automatically. However, for all practical intents and purposes, there is neither point in *completely eliminating* the oscillation nor a technical possibility to accomplish that.

The same principle applies to any self-regulating system. The only thing that fighting self-tuning cycles in excess can do is to ruin the system. It's like fighting a natural phenomenon. Unless you find a way to blow up the Moon out of the sky, there's no way of eliminating tides and ebbs in the oceans. If you are smart enough, you can try to ride them instead—harness their energy and use it to generate electricity, for example. Those ups and downs in capitalist economy are precisely the kind of natural phenomenon that makes capitalism a self-regulating system. People want something they currently don't have?—The increased profit potential immediately attracts capital, which increases production aimed to cover the new demand. We've got a bit too much of the good thing?—The reduced profit margin prompts capital to go looking elsewhere, and any excess automatically vanishes. Of course, any, even the most advanced, super-automated system requires humans to keep an eye on it, to make sure that nothing gets caught, by accident or someone's malice, in its belts and hoses. And that is where the root of all capitalist problems lies. We are never happy with what we have—

at least, not everyone at the same time. And sometimes we rush in too fast and too fervently and improve things a bit too much.

## Socialist Steady Progress

In Marxists' view, one of the reasons socialism is better is that its economy is supposed to develop steadily, according to a centrally devised plan, rather than to be subject to booms and recessions that have been haunting capitalism since the beginning of time. At first glance, indeed, who would dare to deny that never-ending good times sound a lot more inspiring than a sweet candy interlaced with a bitter medicine? But if something looks too good to be true, usually it is. If we remove the splendent wrapping of the eternal socialist prosperity promised by Marxism and take a look at what lies under it …

In theory, it all sounds very sensible and attractive: People, by means of their democratically elected government, set economic goals that will supposedly benefit their entire society. The government plans what and how much to build, produce, and consume. No more capitalist recessions. The economy always, in strict accordance with the plan, goes up, and life of the happy citizens (or should we say, *comrades*?) cheerfully trundles forward. Progress in action. But what about the reality?

Properly planning the entire economy of a large country down to the last nail and rivet is virtually impossible because of the complexity and enormity of this task. Whatever the government plans, some things or other will always go wrong. Even if every single bureaucrat did their utmost, absolute best every time all the time, the sheer scale would guarantee a statistically significant level of failures in one area or another. Making state plans mandatory or providing monetary incentives for fulfilling the plans encouraged enterprise managers in the Soviet Union to be extremely inventive in their reporting techniques. They could almost always juggle numbers to make it look like they had fulfilled their plans, including the times when in fact they had not.

Another common plague of central planning is caused by the desire of high-level officials to show off. Quite often they would come up with overly optimistic, totally unrealistic plans just to look good before their superiors or, at the very top, before the rest of the world. Remember Nikita Khrushchev, the Soviet leader back in 1961, announced the Communist Party's plan to build communism in 20 years, by 1980? Or The Great Leap Forward planned by Chairman Mao in China in 1958 and abandoned in 1961? Both were abject failures. In the Soviet Union, in 1964, three years after his historic announcement at the 22nd congress of the Communist Party, Nikita Khrushchev was deposed from his throne, and the 3rd programme of the Communist Party adopted by the congress was quietly "forgotten." And in China, in the three decades from the 1950s through the 1980s, the only three years when China's economy shrunk instead of growing were precisely the years of The Great Leap Forward. Not to mention tens of millions of additional deaths from famine and repressions that—

by pure coincidence, of course—happened in China at that very time.

In order to be able to sell his product, a capitalist puts it out on the open market, where it faces brutally tough competition. To stand a chance, his product must be noticeably better or cheaper than similar products offered by other capitalists or, at least, appear so in advertisements. Under socialism, there is no market. An enterprise is ordered to make a specific product and to "sell" it to specific consumers at arbitrarily set prices paid in mock money. The product is simply doomed to "succeed" because either no one else is tasked with making it or the overall supply is lagging far behind the demand. No one—neither workers nor designers nor management—has strong enough incentives to make the product better or its production more efficient.

Brainwashing and appealing to one's conscientiousness work only up to a certain point. Why bother trying to do your best if you still get paid pretty much the same money as everyone else around you? Harsh punishments, including jail, possibly torture, or even death, may force you into silent submission but will never force you to come up with innovative ideas or to do more than you are required to. Slavery had already been proven non-viable many times over. Monetary incentives, such as work-based compensation, are not entirely useless, but not nearly as effective as they are under capitalism either. Why?—Because under socialism there is usually not so much for you to spend your money on. The assortment of available consumer goods is rather poor, and their quality is nothing but abysmal. Makes it sort of a catch-22: you have no reason to work too hard because there is nothing much to buy, and there is nothing much to buy because no one is working hard enough.

Also, the Soviet economy had been historically biased towards producing industrial equipment—the heavier, the better—at the expense of consumer goods. At first, at the dawn of the socialist era, the Soviet Union had to build most of its heavy industry from the ground up. A mere couple of decades later it had to repeat the entire process in the western half of their European territory devastated during World War II. Later on, the bias was still intentionally maintained, ostensibly because industrial production made better reports: way more tonnes and roubles than consumer goods would ever be able to show. And there had simply never been enough of anything in the Soviet Union, anyway, and ordinary people had got used to that and were expected to understand … There was also another, more profound and more sinister reason for the never ending lack of consumer goods. We'll explain it later.

## Full Employment

Full employment is another one of the great perks of socialism. Sounds good? Just imagine all the horrors—financial, social, and psychological—of being unemployed under capitalism, and you will never think twice before voting for socialism with both hands. But there's a flip side to it, too. So, you better do think twice before announcing your verdict.

In theory, full employment under socialism—it just happens. The government plans production levels to ensure everyone has a job. In reality, it is virtually impossible to plan it just right. In some areas, there's never enough work force to fill the insatiable black hole of the socialist economy, whereas in others there's an excess, which needs to be put to work. All in all, full employment becomes a goal in itself. In the Soviet Union, the right to work was guaranteed by the Constitution. Anyone deemed to be intentionally dodging employment could be prosecuted and sent to jail. In such an environment, no one had to go out of their way trying to do their job right. Instead, a ubiquitous phenomenon mockingly dubbed Imitation of Blusterous Activity, or IBA, was the name of the game. It was quite common among more professionally-conscious workers to quietly grouch among themselves that a little bit of unemployment would do nothing but good under socialism—to promote personal responsibility in the workplace, they said.

## Chapter 3
# RISE AND FALL OF CLASSIC SOCIALISM

Although terminology is only words, labels that we attach to real things, it is important. Before we discuss something, we need to define what exactly we are going to discuss.

## Terminology

Presently, the term *socialism* refers to two related but nevertheless significantly different concepts. One is the socialism as defined by the Marxist theory. It is a socio-economic formation in which all means of production are owned by the people and the main goal of any business is to produce use-value. Marxism deems this socialism an intermediary phase, a transition from capitalism to communism.

The other meaning that is often attached to the word *socialism* is the type of society that presently exists in western and northern Europe. According to the Marxist classification, this is a form of capitalism because private ownership of means of production still exists, which necessarily implies profit as the primary economic goal of individual businesses. This brand of capitalism features a relatively high degree of government intervention by means of direct government ownership of some enterprises, strict regulations, and a high level of progressive taxation. The government takes away a significant portion of everyone's income and redistributes it throughout the entire society with the goal of equalization—to make rich less rich and to make poor less poor.

The word *progressive* in relation to taxes is a mathematical term and has nothing to do with political progressivism, except that the progressives are proponents of progressive taxation. Progressive taxation means that higher income brackets are taxed at higher rates; the rates increase, or progress, as income grows. The more money you make, the larger portion of it the government takes away. In this manner, a government intentionally discourages high-earners from making too much money. Later on, we'll talk a bit more about this brand of socialism. All we want for now is just to clarify our terminology.

We'll refer to the Marxian type of socialism as classic or true socialism, and we'll label the European-style socialism as social-democratic or socialized capitalism.

A similar discrepancy exists regarding the term *communism*. Those who call the European flavour of capitalism socialism, use the word *communism* to refer to classic socialism. Whereas Marxism defines communism as the next socio-economic formation after classic socialism, the final stage in the development of human society: no countries, no governments, no money, everything is free and abundant, and everyone voluntarily works for free. We'll stick to the Marxist definition of communism, but at the same time we'll honour the historic tradition to refer to governments of truly socialist countries, like the defunct USSR and its former allies, as communist regimes.

Some people might disagree with our definitions or find them controversial; after all, in the Free World, everyone is entitled to have their own opinions. But the labels themselves are unimportant or, more accurately, are not as important as the fact of their existence altogether. We do need some means of referring to the specific types of societies, and generally, we can call anything any way we want, as long as we do that in a clear, unambiguous manner so that everyone understands what exactly we are talking about.

## Rise

Various socialist ideas started emerging around a couple of centuries ago, at about the same time that capitalism became a reality. Some theories suggested that capitalism should be gradually and peacefully transformed into socialism. Others called for a violent revolution: forcible seizure of power; expropriation of all private property without any compensation; and physical extermination of all capitalists, their sidekicks, and all other "enemies of the people." Apparently, a gradual and peaceful transformation presupposes a significant period of time over which the new order comes about. Non-surprisingly, a violent-revolution approach was the first one to materialize.

In March of 1917, in the middle of World War I, a motley alliance of political forces overthrew the Russian monarchy and formed a provisional government. That was meant to be a bourgeois democratic revolution. However, over several months of the ensuing turmoil, the Russian Communists—they called themselves Social Democrats (Bolsheviks) at the time—under the leadership of Lenin, arranged and in early November successfully committed a coup d'état in Saint Petersburg (aka Petrograd at the time), the then Russian capital. They disbanded the newly elected Duma—the Russian parliament—and proclaimed the first ever socialist state of workers and peasants.

The event almost immediately sparked armed opposition, which eventually turned into a full-scale five-year-long civil war. To support their military effort, the Communists established a new order they called War Communism. Everyone was obligated to work for free. Peasants were allowed to keep only the bare-bone minimum of their produce necessary for their physical survival. Everything else was confiscated and distributed for free among workers in cities. The opposition forces, comprised of various factions, lost the war because their mutual political disagreements often precluded proper coordination of their military operations.

Towards the end of the Civil War, it became clear that War Communism was unsustainable as a long-term policy. In 1921, it was replaced with the New Economic Policy, or NEP. A national currency was reinstated, a limited degree of private ownership was allowed, and forcible confiscations of food from peasants were replaced with more reasonable taxes. Many hard-core Communists considered this retraction a treachery of their goals, a step back to capitalism. But Lenin argued it was a necessary measure to invoke speedy recovery of the completely devastated country's economy. Putting complete nationalization on hold allowed the new regime to appear almost civilized and even to attract foreign investments. The latter was especially surprising. International business requires a very significant level of trust. But how can you trust a rogue regime that back in 1917 had renounced all of Russia's international debts as their first order of business? The Communists said their new government was not responsible for whatever money might have been borrowed by the defunct tsarist government. Well, Lenin might have had a point when he said that capitalists would sell you a rope to hang them with. Maybe it wasn't just all trust on their part; maybe it had a greed element built into it too. Or maybe the foreign investors simply had never believed that socialism was viable and thought the NEP was the end of it.

Reportedly, Lenin was planning to keep NEP going for as long as perhaps several decades, until the country's economy became developed enough to smoothly transition to socialism. However, less than three years later, in 1924, Lenin died. His successor, Iosif Dzhugashvili, better known to the world under his alias, Joseph Stalin, started a gradual departure from NEP. In 1928, by when Stalin had defeated most of his political opponents and assumed virtually unrestricted power, he completely abandoned NEP and established a totalitarian regime. He nationalized everything that was still remaining private; kicked out all foreign investors while—naturally—keeping everything they had invested in (so much for their trust!); forced all independent farmers into state-controlled collective farms, or *kolkhozes*; and imposed central planning of the entire economy. Over his 30-year-long reign of terror, tens of millions of people—those very workers and peasants on whose behalf the revolution had been effected—were starved to death; sent to rot in forced-labour prison camps (aka GULAG, the government agency in charge of the camps) in remote regions of Far North, Siberia, and Kazakhstan; or tortured and executed after staged trials or without any legal proceedings altogether. Any whiff of dissent was instantly crushed by the iron blood-stained fist of Stalin's secret police. Lives of most people in the country, including any top-level government officials and even the heads of the secret police itself, were at the whim of this genocidal maniac.

## Totalitarianism

Was Stalinism an unfortunate but only temporary deviation from the road to communism? Was it a rare exception to the general rule? Or is it an intrinsic feature of socialism, the normal condition to which any socialist regime naturally gravitates?

Our analyses are necessarily limited because there simply have not been too many socialist countries around for us to look at. In the course of World War II, Stalin's Soviet Union "liberated" eastern Europe from the German invaders and used its own temporary occupation of those countries to establish communist regimes there in the late 1940s. At about roughly the same time, several countries in eastern Asia joined the communist camp, followed by Cuba in 1959. Those are pretty much the only available historic experiences that we can consider.

The leader of Albanian Communists Enver Hoxha was a great admirer of Stalin. His communist regime in Albania had been terrorizing its people for 40 years until Hoxha finally died in 1985. Hoxha was so unhappy about post-Stalin liberalization, as limited as it was, that he severed all ties with the Soviet Union and called Nikita Khrushchev a revisionist of true Marxism.

The self-proclaimed president-for-life of Romania, Nicolae Ceauçescu, was a hard-core Communist until his last breath. In 1989, the moment the wind of Mikhail Gorbachev's reforms, commonly known in the Soviet Union as *Perestroika*, reached Romania, reverently loving subjects arrested their venerable leader along with his august spouse, put both of them through a speedy three-day trial, and quickly executed them. It should be noted that Ceauçescu was the only one among the fallen Communist leaders of that period who ended up in front of a firing squad at the hands of his very own people. If this is not a sign of how much the Romanians loved their leader, then what is? Interestingly, now, over two decades later, some polls indicate that about a half of the Romanian population appear to be feeling somewhat nostalgic about the Ceauçescu era. This can probably be attributed to the usual difficulties of the transition from a state-run economy to an open market, aggravated by some sort of residual effects of a slave mentality.

Chairman Mao stood at the helm of Communist China for almost 30 years, until his death in 1976. The Chinese history of that period is ripe with all sorts of completely asinine undertakings, accompanied by millions upon millions of people starved to death, executed, driven to suicide, or rotted in prisons and "re-education" camps.

The dynasty of the Kims has been ruling North Korea since the country's inception in 1948. The country is notorious as the last remaining full-scale totalitarian regime on Earth. With a population of less than 25 million, this nuclear power has over one million men in its active-duty army. Probably about the same number of people were starved to death in the last famine that took place about 15–20 years ago. An indirectly estimated number of political prisoners in the country is probably about 200,000.

The Khmer Rouge, the Cambodian Communists, are a somewhat special case; their regime was so terrifyingly bloody that no socialist country wanted to have anything to do with it, at least, not overtly. The Khmer Rouge assumed full power in the country in 1975. Over the following four years of their rule, they systematically exterminated about one quarter of their 8-million population through direct executions and starvation. Soviet news media, which occasionally published materials about what was happening in Kampuchea (that was how the Khmer Rouge renamed Cambodia at the time), was usually careful to avoid mentioning that the Khmer Rouge was, in fact, a communist party. The regime was so brutal that even their next-door neighbours, the Vietnamese Communists, who themselves are not exactly innocent lambs, felt the Khmer Rouge had gone a little too far. The Vietnamese army invaded Cambodia in 1979 and brought down its genocidal regime.

None of the other countries that went through a socialist phase at one point in their history or another were much better than the ones we've just mentioned. They all had their own secret police, often trained by and closely co-operating with the Soviet KGB. None of their Communist rulers tolerated much political opposition. They all jailed, often tortured, and otherwise persecuted anyone whom they suspected of being not overly enthusiastic supporters of the powers-that-be. And of course, none of their peoples were free enough to vote their Communists out.

Clearly, Communists were not the ones who invented the authoritarian form of government, and they were not the only ones who practiced totalitarianism. Brutal dictatorships and genocides are not exactly uncommon in Africa and some other parts of the world. However, nowhere else one can find as high a percentage of repressive regimes as among the countries that were or still are ruled by Communists. So, the quite obvious conclusion that suggests itself is that pretty much all communist movements, once they've come to power, inevitably resort to various forms of coercion. Why would a political party systematically and quite routinely rape its own population? The only answer that makes logical sense is that its policies were hugely unpopular and, therefore, could not be implemented in any way other than by being forced down peoples' throats. More often than not, communist regimes brought about the most disastrous times upon the very people they claimed they strove to make prosper.

## Downfall

Typically, Communists either grabbed power through a violent, bloody uprising or were relatively peacefully installed and subsequently propped up by the Soviet or, in some cases, other Communists.

Once that had been done, the first thing Communists usually did was eliminate any form of opposition. They executed, jailed, exiled, retired, or otherwise neutralized their enemies. Then they donned *hedgehog gloves* (it's a Russian phrase for the opposite of kid gloves) and took a firm grip on all aspects of people's lives, in addition to reshaping everything in the country after their ideals. Except for the Vietnamese ousting the Khmer Rouge from Cambodia in 1979 and the Americans taking out a freshly-baked Stalinist leader in tiny Grenada in 1983, there are no other known cases of toppling a communist regime from without through direct military intervention. Does this mean that once Communists have arrived, they are there for the eternity? That they can't be dealt with by the people of their own country?

After Stalin's death in 1953, his successor, Nikita Khrushchev, somewhat liberalized the Soviet Union. Millions of political prisoners were released from the GULAG, and Khrushchev officially condemned Stalin's cult of personality and his violations of the Party's principle of democratic centralism (the Communists' version of democracy). However, it took several years for all the prisoners to be released, and the condemnation came only in 1956 in a secret speech at the 20th congress of the Communist Party. The general public was informed a whole month later and only of the fact that the speech had been made. The speech itself remained secret for another 33 years—to save face and avoid the embarrassment. According to Khrushchev, the Communist Party did not conspire with Stalin against the people. Rather, claimed Khrushchev, Stalin had temporarily hijacked the Party, which hence was Stalin's victim like everybody and everything else in the country.

In 1964, Leonid Brezhnev managed to retire Khrushchev and, over the 18 subsequent years of his reign, successfully drove the country into what he proudly referred to as the "era of developed socialism" and what ordinary people used to call "overripe stagnation."

The beginning of the end happened in 1985 with the ascension of Mikhail Gorbachev. Reportedly, it was him who first officially characterized Brezhnev's rule as the "era of stagnation." But he merely said publicly what ordinary people had been discussing privately for years. Their collective wit, often augmented by generous doses of vodka—in strict compliance with the ancient Russian tradition—is well known for its unmatched ability to invent funny phrases by combining concepts that normally don't belong together. "Overripe stagnation" is one of such pearls. It means the country had been stagnant all the way round—economically, technologically, socially, intellectually, and psychologically—for so long that the stagnation itself became stagnant. Gorbachev's Perestroika, an attempt to reform the dying regime, was a ghastly example of another bit of folklore: "We wanted as better, but it turned out as usual." Although this aphorism was produced years later, in 1993, by new Russia's then Prime Minister, Victor Chernomyrdin, on an entirely different occasion, it describes Gorbachev's Perestroika just perfectly.

Rather than following the successful example of the Chinese—keep all the power and reshape the economy into anything you want—he chose to start with political liberalization, which immediately backfired. Everything bad that had ever happened in the country since 1917 was the Party's and, hence, Gorbachev's fault. Thus, instead of first trying to consolidate his power, he started up with weakening the leadership position of the Communist Party. However, in a relatively recent interview, Gorbachev still adamantly defended his strategy and blamed its failure on Boris Yeltsin, the first democratically elected President of the Russian Federation, who had harshly criticized Perestroika for its very limited scale, slow pace, and poor planning.

The story goes that as a punishment for the criticism, Gorbachev instigated hounding of Yeltsin and his subsequent removal from the post of First Secretary of the Moscow Communist Party City Committee in 1987. Three years later, Yeltsin officially quit the Communist Party and in 1991 was elected President of Russia, which was one of the 15 union republics that made up the Soviet Union at the time. By then the Soviet Union had already been falling apart, and Yeltsin merely helped it on its way out. So, how could Yeltsin have possibly botched Gorbachev's reforms if he had been out of circulation for most of the four years preceding the Union's official dissolution? But if it was not Yeltsin's scheming, then what exactly brought the *First Country of Victorious Socialism* down? The simple answer is that *socialism doesn't work*; that's the ultimate reason. However, this is not informative enough for anyone to understand what actually happened.

## What Actually Happened

Despite some observers' still believing Gorbachev was a democrat, the reality clearly indicates that he wasn't. He was not planning to transition to a democratic form of government or to market economy; he only wanted to patch up socialism so it could continue lumbering on into communism. By the time Gorbachev came into power, there was not a single sane person in the country who would not admit that the economy was skidding in place, just spinning its wheels and marking time. The most apparent symptom of the disease was severe lack of all sorts of consumer goods and services. Gorbachev decided to fill in the gap by using co-operatives. Historically, Marxism embraced the co-operative form of ownership; so it was ideologically kosher. Gorbachev's original idea was that students and retirees—the only two categories who were officially allowed not to have a state job—would form tiny co-operatively owned businesses, which would provide some limited-scale handy-man services or hand-crafted consumer goods, like shoes or clothes. The co-operatives were mostly meant to only boost people's morale (that is, invoke an emotional reaction: "Oh, finally something has started moving!") without significantly impacting the state-run economy.

Some changes were planned for state-owned enterprises, too. For example, instead of a state plan that had been meant to strain everyone to their physical limits and beyond, businesses would receive state orders for only the stuff that the government deemed vital for the economy. As for the rest of their industrial potential, factories were free to use it as they pleased. Each state-owned enterprise or organization was encouraged to make itself, if not profitable, then at least fiscally solvent. Sounds reasonable? Sounds like a first step towards a market? At first glance—maybe. In reality, however, the concepts of solvency and profitability were utterly meaningless because, in the absence of a free market, all prices were arbitrarily set by the government. And even more importantly, non-cash—one of the two kinds of money in circulation at the time—was not real money. Non-cash was, sort of, Monopoly money that state-owned entities were using for their accounting.

What *is* real money? It's a token, a physical item that, by definition, symbolizes value. To function as money, the item must be universally accepted as a means of payment. The supply of that item must necessarily be limited. Obviously, something that can be easily conjured out of thin air in unlimited quantities does not have real value. Being a physical item is also essential. Electronic money (that is, the money kept in a bank account) is real only if it represents the corresponding amount of physical money; at least, that's how it has always been, so far. Unlike private citizens' savings held in their individual bank accounts, Soviet non-cash was purely electronic; it did not represent cash.

Whatever revenue a factory generated by selling its product was all sent away up the bureaucratic food chain. The product itself was compulsorily assigned to specific buyers at a prescribed price. Whatever input—raw materials and energy—the factory needed for its normal operations it received in accordance with the state plan from its designated suppliers. Once the plan was shaped up, the factory would receive the necessary amount of non-cash money from its commanding chief directorate or ministry. If at any point there was not enough money floating around, the state banks would create, out of nothing, enough to cover the hole.

The same directorate or ministry would also provide enough cash money to the factory to pay its employees. Cash was the second kind of money. It did have *some* value attached to it—the value of the consumer goods and services one could purchase with it. The two kinds of money almost never mingled. Private citizens did not have access to non-cash, and state-owned entities were prohibited from selling any industrial goods for cash and also from buying any consumer goods. Retail stores operated almost exclusively in cash and, as a general rule, were not allowed to sell consumer goods to other state-owned entities, for cash or non-cash—lest some corrupt factory manager bought himself an extra fridge, TV set, or pair of shoes at state's expense.

The moment Gorbachev allowed co-operatives, all those rules instantly changed. Under the new rules, co-operatives were not part of the existing command structure. They were free to produce anything and to sell it to anyone at prices of their own choosing. They were free to hire anyone they wanted for any salary they deemed reasonable and could afford. Co-operatives were never meant to integrate into the mainstream state-owned economy. Therefore, no one thought of squeezing them into the same kind of straightjackets as state enterprises. Such unprecedented level of freedom must have been just an accidental oversight due to lack of experience.

Since co-operatives were not prohibited from dealing with state-owned entities, both had to be able to pay one another. But state enterprises could pay only in non-cash; they were allocated cash strictly for their own employees' salaries. However, despite cash and non-cash being kept isolated from each other, both were operated in the same units—roubles—and the government had never bothered to officially legislate them as *two* separate currencies. Consequently, for co-operatives, there was no difference between cash and non-cash.

For example, suppose an employee of a construction company whose job is to operate an excavator decides to form a co-operative. On a Friday afternoon, he negotiates a deal with his employer, which agrees to lend him the excavator for the weekend, say, for 1,000 roubles per day. Then he goes to the manager of a nearby factory that is building a new shop and, therefore, needs to do some digging. The manager jumps at the opportunity to save some of the factory's non-cash funds (he is required to make profit now, remember?) by paying the co-operative only a fraction of the officially approved cost. What makes the savings possible is the historically formed significant differences in the scales of cash and non-cash money, sometimes up to several orders of magnitude. All salaries and consumer-goods prices had always been kept very low, typically within a ceiling of a few hundred roubles, whereas state-owned enterprises routinely operated in millions upon millions. So the manager knows that even if he pays only a fraction of the official price for the digging, it's still going to be a lot of money for a private individual. The manager and the co-operative sign a contract for 10,000 roubles to be paid out in return for a certain amount of digging done over the weekend. On Monday morning, satisfied with the job done, the manager authorizes a transfer of 10,000 roubles from his factory's bank account to the co-operative's bank account. The co-operator pays 2,000 to the construction company that owns the excavator and pays the remaining 8,000 to himself as salary. With a linear 13-percent income tax rate, the operator pockets nearly 7,000 roubles. He repeats this cycle a couple more times, and by the end of the month he's made so much money that he almost forgets to pick up his 300-rouble official monthly salary for his work on weekdays!

Until that point, the total amount of cash in circulation had been very tightly controlled by the High Command. With the advent of co-operatives, the ocean of non-cash became directly connected to the teeny-weenie pond of cash.

In an instant, all sorts of private businesses materialized out of thin air. Anyone with an ounce of entrepreneurial spirit immediately rushed in to tap into the unlimited supply of non-cash, which could now be almost effortlessly converted into cash. The obvious and the only possible outcome of that galactic-scale imbalance between the amount of money and the amount of consumer goods available for sale was a significant jump in prices. Co-operatives started buying out all merchandise they could find, at low state prices, directly from manufacturers, often even before the stuff was produced, and selling it in their privately-owned stores for several times its official retail price. The government tried to level the field by raising the official prices, but the increase did not go far enough and its effect was like piling up a dozen sandbags in a hope they'll stop a tsunami.

Gorbachev dashed in to put out the fire. First his government jacked up personal income tax rates, leaving the original 13-percent rate in effect for only up to 700 roubles per month. Co-operators reacted to that by "hiring" new employees whose only "job" was to allow their names to be used in payroll registers in exchange for a small compensation. That tactic of ostensibly distributing large cash payouts among large numbers of "employees" kept everyone's salaries within the lowest tax bracket.

Having failed to legitimately curb co-operatives' earnings, the government decided to approach the problem from a different angle. In January of 1991, it launched a surprise monetary reform—a variation of the classic stunt that had been successfully pulled off several times since 1917. Different in their individual specifics, all those reforms had the same ultimate goal: to reduce the people's purchasing power or, put simply, to rip everyone off. Since the government couldn't increase production of consumer goods to the level that would match the amount of cash in circulation, the excess cash had to be eliminated directly. High-denomination banknotes were to be removed from circulation within three days and were to be replaced with new ones at a later time. The general idea was to make the exchange of old bills so difficult that many people wouldn't be able to make it within the allotted time frame and would therefore lose their cash. "Normal" people were not expected to have much cash; hence those who had lots of it were, by definition, bad people and it was OK if they lost some of their "unearned" money. To further curb people's spending, the monetary reform was followed by draconian restrictions on the amount of cash citizens were allowed to withdraw from their bank accounts. In the country where cheques were almost unheard of, where credit or debit cards did not exist, and where all consumer purchases were paid in cash, restricting access to cash was a very big deal. However, the sharp end of those measures turned out to be grossly misplaced. Instead of co-operators, who held most of the existing cash, it were rank-and-file citizens who were hit the hardest; they didn't have much savings and, therefore, had trouble hanging on while waiting to be compensated for the surrendered now-invalid banknotes. Co-operators, on the other hand, had easy back-door access to banks and quietly exchanged all their high-denomination cash within the first few hours from the moment the reform had been officially announced or, in many cases, even prior to that.

Another old-time trick was to suspend the state-issued bonds. And again, ordinary citizens were the ones left holding the bag full of now virtually worthless paper. Co-operators hadn't had much time to develop enough trust in the Communist leadership and, therefore, hadn't invested much in the bonds.

The total amount of cash soaked up by all those rip-offs was like a few bucketfuls scooped up from the ocean. And it was nothing compared to the popular uproar they caused and a complete loss of any remnants of credibility by the Communist leadership.

To make the bad situation worse, one of Gorbachev's most brilliant ideas of the time was to launch a campaign against the most revered ancient Russian tradition of heavy drinking. No sooner did he mention in one of his public speeches that drinking was bad, as his overzealous lackeys rushed to uproot vineyards, scrap entire bottle-manufacturing plants, and cut production of all booze. A mere few months later lines for vodka stretched out for kilometres, and neither doubling nor even quadrupling the prices could alleviate the demand. The lack of booze led to two major consequences: the sober Ivans were a lot more danger to the regime than drunk, and the cash not spent on vodka became "hot." Hot cash burns its owner's hands, demanding to be spent. If there are not enough consumer goods to spend it on, prices jump right into the stratosphere and social pressures rise to explosive levels. Lulled by the fact that until then, for the last 75 years, the Communists had been able to get away with virtually anything, Gorbachev didn't realize that it was not a very good time for enforcing sobriety.

The only possible way to fix the fiscal situation that had gone completely out of hand was to relinquish government control over prices altogether. The idea was to issue an official blessing to a complete merger between cash and non-cash, the process that had already been underway for quite some time. The rouble would be allowed to plummet into an abyss and to keep falling until it reached a hard floor—its real market value. All prices would instantly skyrocket. Many state-owned enterprises would go bankrupt, and a whole lot of people would find themselves below the poverty line. Over the preceding 40 years or so, this approach, known as *shock therapy*, had been rather successfully tried on multiple occasions around the world. The most well-known examples are post–World War II West Germany in 1948, Chile after the military coup in 1975, New Zealand in 1984, Bolivia in 1985, and post-Communist Poland in 1989.

Gorbachev was ideologically unprepared to take this step, because it would signify a de facto introduction of a free-market system—capitalism. Gorbachev's popular support had been dwindling, and most likely his regime would not have survived the shock therapy, anyway.

In August of 1991, in a state of utter panic, the Inner Party hardliners effected a coup d'état (the Russians called it the August Putsch), the last desperate attempt to turn back the clock. They formed an Emergency State Committee, put Gorbachev under house arrest, and declared his authority suspended "for health reasons." However, it's been a long time since anyone in the country had tried anything that radical. The conspirators proved totally out of practice. First of all, they didn't have the guts to kill Gorbachev and thereby preclude any chance of his return to power. On the contrary, it looked like they might still be counting on his personal clout, hoping that, faced with a *fait accompli* (an accomplished fact, a done deal—in proper English), he might come to his senses and join them, making their power grab look legitimate. Their second and, as it turned out, the decisive error was their failure to neutralize Yeltsin, who at the time of the coup was already the legitimate President of Russia. Not only was he left alive, but he even dodged an arrest and successfully headed popular opposition. Although Yeltsin and Gorbachev had been at odds with each other from almost the very beginning of Perestroika, their political differences were mainly about how far and how fast Perestroika should go. The putschists, on the other hand, were against Perestroika altogether. Yeltsin, being a proponent of more radical reforms than Gorbachev, presented a greater danger to the putschists.

The failed coup precipitated the inevitable. After the coup had been defeated, Gorbachev was restored to power, but only nominally. By the end of 1991, all 15 of the constituent Soviet republics formally announced their independence and the dissolution of the Union. Gorbachev became the President of a no longer existing entity and had no choice but to take his retirement.

Further to the question of what exactly caused the collapse of the Soviet Union, we should look back at the beginning of Chapter 1. All the political struggle, the Communists' ploys to stay in power, and the pressure put by the opposition forces on the incumbents—all that bustle was only the tip of the iceberg, the ideological superstructure on top of the economic foundation. That's how the Marxist theory explains social phenomena. In a funny sort of way, Marxism appears to be right on the mark here. Whatever the specific political circumstances may have been at the time, the existing order of things in the country's economy simply could no longer function. Everything else—the dissolution of the Union and the Communists' loss of power—was corollary to that.

As for the Eastern Bloc countries, they had no viability of their own; they significantly depended both economically and politically on the Soviet Union. They all kicked their respective buckets a year or two before the end of the Soviet Union, as soon as Mikhail Gorbachev—his hands too full with Perestroika to worry about their problems—pulled the plug on them.

# Chapter 4
# AROUND THE WORLD

Being the first ever country ruled by Communists, the Soviet Union had always been the centre of gravity for Communists and all sorts of Leftist movements across the world. It didn't take long for the Soviet Communists to penetrate and subordinate their international counterparts and sympathizers.

## Ripples and Fallouts

In the first years of their reign, the Soviet Communists were mostly working towards instigating Communist-led revolutions in other countries. They were worried about the fate of their own regime and hoped that breaking the imperialists' ranks would ensure their own survival. They were so desperate that Stalin even supported Adolf Hitler's regime in Germany until the very moment German tanks crossed the Soviet border in June of 1941.

When you come to think of it, Stalin's mistaking Hitler for an ally is not all that surprising. There is some confusion about Hitler's exact place on the political map. On one hand, his party was called National *Socialist*. Some stunning similarities between Stalin's and Hitler's policies, including even almost identical propagandist posters, cause some observers to claim that Hitler should be classified as an extreme Left. However, taking into account that ownership of production means largely remained private, Marxists put Hitler among the extreme Right in an attempt to distance themselves from his horrendous atrocities. This scholastic discrepancy can be easily resolved and everything can be made to look logical if, instead of imagining the political spectrum as a straight line, we visualize it as a circumference, with the political Centre straight in front of us. The visible 90-degree arc to the left of the Centre is where the "normal" Left live, and the visible arc to the right of the Centre is where the "normal" Right live. The invisible, back half of the circumference hosts the "ultras": on the left we have the ultra-Left, and on the right we have the ultra-

Right. Thus the extreme Left and the extreme Right come together at the farthest point from us on our circular model.

With Stalin more than half-way behind the Left horizon and with Hitler all the way back to the Right, they were indeed very close politically, which, however, did not prevent them from clashing headlong. The fact that the Soviets won is not surprising at all and is far from proving communism's superiority over Nazism. The Soviets were defending their homeland against the German invaders, and quite naturally, they preferred to remain slaves of their own monster rather than to let him be replaced with a foreign one. The victory gave the Soviets a unique opportunity to expand their domain. Since Germany didn't have a common border with the Soviet Union, the Soviets had a valid reason to fight their way to Berlin through most of eastern Europe. At first, their purported allies—the Americans, the Canadians, and the British— were not in any rush to interfere in the squabble between the two worst bad guys of the century. The more Hitler and Stalin pummeled each other, the better off the Free World would be. But when the Soviets started prevailing, the "allies" immediately opened the Second Front and fought their way to Berlin from the west, lest the Communists took over all of Europe.

In the few following years, Stalin brought Communists to power in all the countries the Soviets had "liberated" from Hitler. There happened a few hiccups on the thorny path to eternal happiness. In 1956, the Hungarians tried to oust their Communists, but only to be flattened out by Soviet tanks. Something similar transpired in 1968 in Czechoslovakia. After Stalin's death in 1953, the Albanian dictator Enver Hoxha severed all ties with the Soviet Union and cursed Khrushchev for abandoning Stalinism. The Yugoslavian Communists under the leadership of Marshall Josip Broz Tito liberated their country from Hitler on their own and thus avoided Soviet occupation. Tito chose to build a different version of socialism in Yugoslavia; it was more like a mixed-market model with emphasis on co-operative forms of ownership. Tito ignored Stalin's displeasure and managed to keep Yugoslavia more or less independent from the rest of the socialist camp.

Apart from those few mishaps, the Soviets had effectively ruled half of Europe. All Communist leaders in those Eastern Bloc countries were merely puppets controlled from Moscow. When Gorbachev started his Perestroika, he slackened his grip on eastern Europe, and all communist regimes there started toppling even before the Soviet Union itself collapsed. What does this tell us? An answer that seems obvious is that Communists never had genuine popular support; all they could do was forcibly seize power when such an opportunity presented itself and then physically suppress any dissent. The moment their grip on people's throats slackened, they were immediately kicked out. In other words, communist regimes are intrinsically oppressive and, contrary to their claims, are opposed to the will of the people.

Not everyone agrees with this conclusion. In a futile attempt to save face after the crash of the Soviet Union, some adherents of Marxism are trying to explain away the entire history of the Soviet Union by allusions to various relatively minor circumstances that caused some unfortunate decisions, unforeseen turns, and other specific irregularities eventually resulting in distortions of true Marxism. They claim, Stalin only used Marxism-Leninism as a *fig leaf*, that he wasn't a Marxist at all. In their view, he was just a very bad guy with an unmatched knack for bureaucratic games. Stalin, they go on, replaced devoted communists with apolitical careerists, skillfully installed them into key positions, and then commanded them as he pleased. Those career-conscious bureaucrats effectively sold their loyalty for privileged positions and material gains. Those people had nothing to do with Marxism. In fact, their mindset was purely capitalistic. Following this line of "reasoning," it wouldn't be too far off to imagine that we might eventually reach the point of absurdity, where Stalinism could be portrayed as a form of capitalism.

Well, nice try, *comrades*. Such attempts to whitewash Marxism are resemblant of a joke from the gentlemen's series. What would a Farmer Joe do if he accidentally stepped into a cow cake?—He would clean himself up and be on his way. And what would a Gentleman do if *he* happened to step into the same spot?—He would pretend that the stink was emanating from someone else. So, maybe those comrades are gentlemen?

It appears that communist regimes have never been legitimately voted into power. Why? Unfair voting rules? Not likely. Generally, bourgeois democracies allow for multiple political parties to compete. Then how come almost no one wants Communists to win? Is it because most of the people are too stupid to figure out on their own what's good for them? Was *that* why Communists always felt it was their duty to seize power by force?

Let's try another angle. Is *compromise* a dirty word? It looks like for Communists it is. Most of the rest of the political spectrum can usually agree upon at least *something*. With only a couple of exceptions (the former Yugoslavia and modern China), Communists always regarded anything that involved private ownership of productive means as mudding the purity of their goals. Could this be why the one-party system is their all-time favourite? If their promises of a better life were true, shouldn't they allow the reality to speak for itself? Instead of physically eliminating all opposition, why not simply let it die out naturally?

Anyway, whatever theories one might fancy—in *our* world, everyone still has the right to do so—it is a fact that nothing good has come out from communist regimes, so far, in the sense that the overall quality of life of ordinary people in the former and in a few still remaining countries of classic socialism has always been significantly lower than in comparable capitalist countries. It is also a fact that a vast majority of ordinary people don't support Communists, don't want them in power, and eventually get rid of them wherever Communists happen to grab power without asking.

# China

After much fighting—all sorts of revolutions, counterrevolutions, and wars—the country eventually fell under Communist rule in 1949. The leader, Mao Tse-tung, aka Mao Zedong, or simply Chairman Mao, had super-ambitious plans that swayed to the Left of mainstream Marxism. He wanted to skip capitalism and socialism and jump into communism directly from feudalism. Instead, in the best traditions of totalitarianism—he outdid perhaps even Uncle Joe (the westernized nickname of Joseph Stalin)—Mao successfully ruined whatever little the devastated country still had after all of its preceding interesting times. His three most notable accomplishments were agricultural communes in the early 1950s, the Great Leap Forward in 1958–1961, and the Cultural Revolution in 1966–1976. The communes eliminated traditional families and, combined with the Leap and ubiquitous repressions, caused a big-time famine. The Cultural Revolution, which boiled down to instigating pervasive political purges throughout the entire society and to aggrandizement of Mao, plunged the much-suffered country into unimaginable anarchy and would have completely destroyed it had Chairman Mao not died in 1976. The total death toll of this quarter-century adventure is in the order of tens of millions, perhaps up to 65 million, according to some indirect estimates.

Many communist parties of today are going out of their way to distance themselves from such doom-and-gloom. They argue that Stalinism, Maoism, and all other known flavours of totalitarianism are not representative of true Marxism and are its aberrations. Stalin and Mao, on the other hand, both claimed themselves the purest breed of Marxists and used to get along with each other very nicely. After Stalin's death, Chairman Mao and Nikita Khrushchev denounced *each other* as revisionists of true Marxism.

After Mao had died, the new leadership of the Communist Party of China turned out to be a lot more pragmatic. Their motto was, "Who cares if a cat is black or white, as long as it catches the mice." Without letting even the tiniest crumb of political power out of their hands, they started a very deliberate, gradual shift towards capitalism. Communism still remaining their official goal, state capitalism became their practical reality. Over the following three decades, the Chinese economy averaged 10-percent annual growth and is now the second largest economy in the world, ceding only to the USA.

The transformation still far from being over, there are already quite a few tell-tales of upcoming troubles, but China is yet another example of a communist regime harnessing some form of capitalism to pull its economy out of a hole. The future of China is not set, Communists are still in power, but it's doubtful that after getting their first taste of a better life the Chinese will want to abandon it in favour of some hazy idea of communism. Most likely, it will be a few more decades before the Communists relinquish their exclusive position and dissipate into a pluralistic political background.

## European Socialism

Most countries in western and northern Europe are often referred to as socialist because their policies are geared towards equalizing outcome rather than opportunity. This type of society doesn't quite fall under the Marxist definition of socialism, because private ownership of means of production has not been rooted out yet and profit is still driving the economy. Lenin regarded proponents of building socialism through peaceful gradual reforms as petty-bourgeois elements not fit to lead the working class to the bright future of communism. Earlier we stipulated that we'd call the European brand of socialism social-democratic or socialized capitalism. Don't read too much into these terms; we have introduced them merely for the sake of clarity and convenience—just to indicate that those European countries are not in the same league as the former Soviet Union and its Eastern Bloc allies.

What's so remarkable about the European social-democratic countries? On one hand, their economies are based on capitalism—to varying degrees. On the other hand, their political leaders call themselves socialists—again, of varying flavours. Their main goal is to enforce universal equality among all the people. Those countries are often dubbed *welfare states* because the state is responsible for everyone's welfare. Those who have jobs or private businesses earn their own living and, through taxes, pay for the less fortunate, who for various reasons don't work. At first glance, all this looks very nice, warm, and fuzzy, but that's the Left's traditional trademark. Their rhetoric always sounds very humane, friendly, and therefore attractive to those who rarely bother to switch on any significant portions of their brains. Reality, however, often bites.

If everyone is pretty much guaranteed an apartment to live in and money to live on, why would anyone want to seek a job? Just because staying at home is too boring? What's the point of expending your blood, sweat, and tears if half of what you earn goes to your neighbour who doesn't lift a finger? Why would you risk your personal life savings to run a business if you can't make a decent profit because most of your revenue is lost to taxes? Whatever remains is not much more than what you are paying your employees, who are not risking anything. Perhaps, you'll do all that out the goodness of your heart; after all, aren't we all *equal*? So, the very first snag in this socio-economic model is lack of motivation for anyone to do anything. The more socialized a country is, the less the motivation is. But motivation is a purely psychological factor, isn't it? Can't it be overcome, for example, through targeted official propaganda or peer pressure? Shouldn't every responsible society member disregard any monetary disincentives and happily rush to work simply because they realize that, to be consumed, any wealth must first be produced?—Maybe in a Utopia. But in real life, responsible, hard-working members of the society feel robbed, exploited, perhaps even enslaved by their "comrades" who enjoy the same guaranteed equal outcome for free. So the next "logical" step along this road is to *force* everyone to work—you know, like Stalin and Mao did it in their time. Lacking financial incentives, how else can you ensure there are enough sloggers around to support the rest of the comrades?

But the Europeans wouldn't do that; they are *good* guys—you know, in white hats. Without coercion, the only other way to make people work is to still maintain some degree of inequality so that those who work would have more than those who don't. That means taxation must be kept at a low enough level to make having a job or running a business financially worthwhile. The overall volume of direct handouts and social services must be kept within available means and should not be borrowed from future generations. Can this kind of balance be attained and then consistently sustained? The easiest way to get an answer to this question without drowning in all sorts of calculations and speculations is to look at what's going on in Europe.

Greece has been the first among the European welfare states to face the music. In a democratic society, governments periodically change. One government borrows as much money as it can spend in pursuit of its socialist vision. The more voters get more freebies, the better. A few years later, another government points its finger at the politicians who are no longer around as the ones responsible for having put the country into a debt pit. It promises to fix the problem and borrows more money to pay for the previous government's debts. In the meantime, the country's population has grown and more money is needed to keep everyone happy. So the government has no choice but to borrow some more. Then yet another government comes, blames its predecessors for all the fiscal troubles, and … claims more borrowing is vital to ensure the country can keep going.

Greece has been cooking its books to cover up its excessive borrowing. But no one can keep borrowing forever; at some point debts *must* be repaid, lest the country lose its creditworthiness. Being a member of the euro currency zone, Greece cannot arbitrarily print money to pay for its socialism. So, eventually, it had to go around, cap in hand, begging to be bailed out of its fiscal predicament. In return for emergency loans, Greece has been forced to shed some of its fat. But the Greeks have got used to working less and receiving more. They consider government's handouts their natural rights. Faced with severe austerity measures, the Greeks embarked on a never-ending rampage of strikes, violent protests, and calls for quitting the euro zone and printing as much drachmas as they need.

Spain is merrily trudging right behind Greece. On top of its generous social perks, Spain had recently gone through a green gauntlet. Around the dawn of the new millennium, the Spanish Socialists decided to force Spain into the green world of the future. They provided billions upon billions in subsidies to paint their energy green. Each green job they created killed on average 2.2 jobs in other industries. Although some Greens are pointing out that 20-percent unemployment is not the highest level in Spain's history, it's hardly a sign of success either. Anyway, the Greens can juggle any numbers they want and pretend the programme worked, but faced with the unflinching reality of the national debt going over 270 percent of GDP, Spain recently had no choice but to pull the plug on its green initiatives. Austerity measures will definitely hurt and spark massive protests, but ... After all, the Spaniards themselves voted for their Socialist government; why should they be allowed to wriggle their way out of footing their own bill?

Portugal is yet another example of failed socialist policies. Italy's finances are in no better shape. Cyprus is being bailed out as these words are being written. Denmark is trying to spend its way out of an impending Greece-style debt trap. Can you dig your way out of a pit? Overall, at least half of the socialized Europe is already in hot water, and the other half is not too far behind.

## Chapter 5
# LEFT VS. RIGHT

Mimicry is a biological phenomenon consisting in that species of one type (mimics) possess characteristics, such as appearance, scent, or behaviour, that make them similar to species of another type (models). The similarities confuse predators or other natural enemies (dupes) and thus increase mimics' chances of survival.

## Mimicry

Socialist and communist experiments have been failing time after time. Those Left regimes that tried to save themselves inevitably ended up re-introducing some forms of capitalism and, eventually, the Left either lost their political power altogether or had to give up their privileged positions and share power with other parties. Given virtually a 100-percent rate of failure, how come they never stop trying? How come they are even still around? Don't they realize their cause is doomed? Don't they ever learn from history? The main reason the Left never die out is that *We, The People* keep playing into their hand. It's *us* who should pay more attention to history lessons. As long as we are willing to listen to their sweet talk, there'll always be enough politicians trying to play us like a violin.

Does it mean we are all hopelessly stupid?—Well, not entirely. After 75 years of the Soviet Union, most of us *have* learned something. We do know that Communists are *bad*—well, sort of. Unfortunately, most of the time, it's not real knowledge based on historic facts but rather some sort of residual subconscious perception based on bits and pieces of various rumours and legends flying around. But even *that* helps. In virtually any country of the Free World, any political party whose name includes any form of the word *communist* is pretty much doomed to a ghostly half-life in the political backyard. But …

… we haven't earned the right to rejoice yet. Devout communists are tough and devious. Such a minor setback as the crash of their "Holy Land"—the former Soviet Union—wouldn't stop them from ploughing on. But what can they do if *everyone* knows their hats are black? That's no problem for a determined marketing pro: if you can't get in through the front door, then go through the back; if you can't get in through the back door, go through a window. The recipe is unbelievably simple: re-wrap and rename. They'll just form new parties or penetrate and gradually take over existing parties that don't have the word *communist* in their names. They put on white hats and momentarily get lost in a swarm of parties to the left of the Centre. Some of the tell-tale keywords to look for are *socialist, democratic, progressive, liberal* and all possible combinations thereof, often also featuring the word *new* squeezed in here or there. The more there are parties whose names include a word or two from this list, the easier it is for communists to hide in their midst.

Hold on a sec, if the word *communist* indeed raises a big red flag, then why still *are* there parties that are named Communist? Why wouldn't they just quietly disappear and wait for people to forget about them? But no, they are left lingering in the background of political obscurity for a reason (Tough and devious—remember?). Those Communist parties serve a very important purpose—diversion. If they went away altogether, some of us might get suspicious and might start snooping around to see whether communists had gone back underground—you know, like switching to full conspiracy mode and plotting another world revolution. Once we started looking for them, it would be just a matter of time before someone recognized them and thus rendered their disguise useless. But with an openly existing Communist Party, we are a lot more likely to overlook their masquerading comrades virusing their way through sister parties. Most modern-day communists are now wearing white hats, call themselves socialists or democrats of one flavour or another, and do whatever else it takes to look sufficiently decent, presentable, and harmless, so that Left-minded voters would have no second thoughts about them. (Do you want to play a game? Guess which political party has recently removed all explicit references to the word *socialism* from its charter in an attempt to gain more parliamentary seats in the next federal elections?) Once elected, they'll continue their masquerade for as long as they need, until they are ready for another Big Bang. In the meantime, they'll erode everything they touch—bit by bit, brick by brick—until it's too late for us to vote them out.

## Rise of the Left

In the recent years the Left have been gaining strength and influence all over the world. Even in America, the country that is supposed to be the bulwark of freedom, the guiding star of the Free World, the Left are prevailing at this point in history. However strange it might seem, the demise of the Soviet Union has boosted their popularity and influence. During the Cold War, the world was pretty much black-and-white: if you are not with *us*, then you are with *them*; any hat that was not white was officially declared black. No grey was tolerated in-between. With communism in the former Soviet Union and Eastern Bloc officially defeated and with black hats no more, we are no longer afraid to wander off our snowy white reservation into adjacent lands of grey. In other words, we now don't mind listening to what the Left have to say. There is no danger in it, is there? After all, they are *not* Communists.

Capitalism is not nice and smooth; it does have a few rough edges. Its economic cycles, with a constant, ubiquitous fear of unemployment and poverty always hanging over our heads, are not something that we are entirely comfortable with. It's in our human nature to always try to improve everything. We wouldn't knowingly vote for replacing capitalism with classic socialism, but why not change a little bit of this and regulate a tiny piece of that, and maybe life will become better and merrier? And the Left are only too happy to hold their lamp for us and lure us into *their* path.

Their ideas always sound extremely attractive to our softened hearts:

"Poverty is awful; let's spread some wealth around ..."

"Let's increase the minimum wage so that it will become possible to actually live on it ..."

"Leaving people out in the streets is inhumane; let's give everyone a cheap apartment or, better still, a house ..."

"Owning a house is more than just the American dream; it's a human right ..." ... *as is high-speed Internet access* ...

"We owe our seniors; let's give them enough pensions to live out their golden years in dignity ..."

"Denying our fellow humans medical help just because they don't have money to pay for it is beyond outrageous; let's make healthcare free for all ..."

"Education is a key to the future; let's make sure everyone gets a university degree ..."

This list can go on and on *ad infinitum*; wherever you look, there is always something we can improve, someone we can help.

Of course, we should try to improve and to help, no argument about that. The question is *how*?

With almost any social or economic issue, there is always head butting between what appears to be an intuitive and reasonable solution coming from the Left and a path suggested by the Right that, at first glance, might seem to be leading in the wrong direction. Let's take a quick look at a few randomly picked examples—just to get the general idea.

How to help the poor?

"Let's raise the minimum wage," say the Left, "make sure one can actually live on it."

"Legislating a higher minimum wage," object the Right, "is a sure way to kill small businesses, which provide more than half of all jobs. What would you prefer: to have a job for a wage that you can't live on or to have a law that makes the wage livable but to lose the job that pays it? Let the market decide what each job is worth. It's the only way this can work."

"Greedy capitalists will never voluntarily cut into their profits," respond the Left. "The minimum wage is too important to be left at the mercy of unpredictable market forces; it's our moral duty as humans to legislate humane conditions for our fellow humans."

"The poor need more social programmes," claim the Left. "Let's raise taxes on the rich. They can afford to pay more."

"Then they'll have less money left to expand their businesses," point out the Right. "There'll be fewer jobs for the poor, less profits for the rich, and hence, less taxes for you. Let's *cut* taxes, and the tax revenue will *increase*."

"Nonsense," sneer the Left. "How can we get more by taking less? We can't afford to *pay for tax cuts*."

"It's not like you would be giving away *your* money," argue the Right. "When you cut taxes, people keep more of *their* money."

"But it's the rich we are talking about; they don't need more money. Anyway, even if we won't get more revenue, we still should raise taxes on the rich—just for the sake of fairness."

"Healthcare is an essential human right," assert the Left. "Everyone must receive the same level of medical services regardless of how rich or poor they are."

"Our natural rights don't come from a government," explain the Right. "They come from a higher authority. And healthcare is a privilege, not a right."

This drives the Left into a righteous frenzy. "Life *is* a natural right," they reason, "and medicine is essential for maintaining it."

"But medicine does not happen naturally—like, for example, the babies we produce; it comes from doctors, who need to be paid for their work."

"Wherever it comes from, all humans are entitled to have it. We'll tax the rich to pay the doctors to treat everyone the same," promise the Left.

"You can't tax enough for that," warn the Right, "because medicine is way too expensive. Presently, only the poor are not getting the full service, but when you start rationing it, *all* of us will end up with substandard healthcare."

"At least, it will be fair; everyone will be getting the same," shrug it off the Left with a sly grin.

"We must improve living conditions for the poor," announce the Left. "Let's force banks to give mortgages to everyone, so everyone can realize their American dream."

"But if they are poor, how are they going to pay their mortgages back? They'll lose their homes, banks will lose their money, and we—that is, *all* of us—will end up paying the price for your idealistic nonsense."

"Well, capitalism can't exist without periodic crises, anyway. You should be used to them by now. What does it matter if you have to weather one more?"

mischievously smile the Left.

"This is not going to be a regular recession cycle," gloomily predict the Right. "When banks start falling, the entire system can collapse."

"No problem, gloat the Left, we'll build a new-and-improved one; it's called socialism. What's the point of having your capitalism if it can't provide a decent living for everyone?"

There is no end to such examples. You can name almost *any* issue, and you'll find the Left and the Right on the opposite sides of it. At first glance, the solutions coming from the Left always look more intuitive, reasonable, and attractive—that is, before you bother to dig under their shiny surface. Unfortunately, for many of us, it's easier *not* to bother. It's a lot harder to swallow the bitter medicines that the Right put forward. Their solutions usually appear contrary to common sense: How is it possible to help the poor by giving them less? How can you collect more tax revenue by cutting taxes? How can we have more freedom without having a huge government to protect it?

We, humans, are supposed to use our brains not just as a counter-balance to our butts that keeps the body's centre of gravity in its proper position. We must learn to see beyond the first glance. More guns doesn't necessarily mean more violence. Look at countries like Israel or Switzerland, where nearly every household has firearms. No one's going around there shooting people for target practice. More money for the poor *perpetuates* poverty instead of reducing it. More government usually means *less* freedom. Market forces are not an invention of the Right; they are a natural phenomenon. Trying thoughtlessly to put a halter on them is virtually guaranteed to come back biting us in the you-know-what. But the Left don't seem to mind experimenting; after all, it's mostly *our* you-know-whats they are putting in the line of fire, not just *theirs*.

Most of us are so busy trying to earn a living that we don't have time or energy left to think about much else.

"Politics is a dirty business," we say. "The Right politicians are in no way better than the Left ones. To hell with all of them; let them fight it out among themselves. Leave us alone; we have enough problems of our own."

Those of us who support the Right are too complacent to believe that the Left present any real danger, while the Left are quietly chiselling away our breathing space, crumb by crumb, until we've all been herded into a paddock with a sign "2084" on its gates.

## Pendulum

*Pendulum effect* is just a descriptive term for a concept that is discussed in this section. It has not been inspired by and is in no way related to any political-pendulum theories that might be in existence elsewhere.

The American two-party political system looks as if it were specifically designed for the pendulum effect. However, this phenomenon equally applies to all countries.

If the pendulum is on the Left, when the incumbents screw up, it swings to the Right. When the Right go out of favour, the pendulum swings back to the Left. Tic–tock, Left–Right, Right–Left. The flow of political logic, or lack thereof, from the Left: more social entitlements and services for the people—more spending—a bigger government—again, more spending—budget deficits—higher national debt—higher tax rates—stalling economy and lower tax revenues—more deficits—even higher tax rates—... a swing of the pendulum. Then come the Right and reverse the trend: lower tax rates to revive the economy—less spending to curb budget deficits—smaller government—less entitlements and services—more unhappy voters—... another swing of the pendulum.

But the process is not exactly symmetric: the length of the Left arc is not the same as that of the Right one.

The Left have always been fixated on the idea of redistribution of wealth: taking away from the rich and giving it to the poor. As soon as they are voted into power, they rush to tax the rich. The rich have less money left to invest in business. The economy takes a nosedive, people lose jobs and become unhappy. Increasing tax rates doesn't result in increased tax revenues. Consequently, the Left are unable to deliver on their promises to take care of ordinary folks. They just screw everything up, get their well-deserved kick in the butt, and leave their mess for their successors to mop up. Then come the Right and try to unscrew everything back. However, fixing is always harder than screwing up. Blowing up a house in a spectacular firework might take just a few seconds and gather crowds of cheering onlookers, but afterwards no one would be voluntarily hanging around for months to watch the house being rebuilt. Even less likely are they to stick around for years that it would take for life of the residents of the said house to return to normal. People get bored and start looking for other entertainment. With each swing of the pendulum, the mess inherited by the Right is inevitably getting bigger and it's increasingly harder to convince people to keep tightening their belts with no happy end in sight. Afraid of losing their electability, the Right have to loosen a few nuts here and there and eventually end up sliding to the Left. Thus the pendulum spends increasingly more time on the Left than on the Right. If this trend continues, at some point the Left will be able to trick the pendulum to always stay on their side and never cross back into the Right zone.

## Destination

It's time now for us to return to our original question, *Where are we, as a society, heading?* No one knows the exact future; no one can definitively tell where we'll eventually end up or whether there even *is* a specific destination to our journey. What we *can* do is predict with a reasonable degree of certainty where our current road is leading. If we all like that place, we can stay on course and enjoy the ride. But if some of us would rather go elsewhere, now may be a good time to do something about it. Our future is not set; we are not doomed to arrive at a predetermined point no matter what we do. Karl Marx and his theories notwithstanding, it *is* in our power to plot our own course, and for that, knowing our current coordinates and the direction in which we are moving is essential.

The actual history of humankind has never been a smooth sailing in one direction. There were periods when we straggled off course or even doubled back. But if we look at the big picture, so far, we've been invariably progressing to the Left. Let's travel this path and enjoy its attractions. It will be more demonstrative, instead of travelling along the Time axis, with all the higgledy-piggledy deviations and course changes, to take our imaginary trip only along the political spectrum and not focus on the timing more than necessary.

Earlier we suggested that the real-life political spectrum more conveniently maps to a circumference than to a straight line. A straight-line model starts at the point of the political Centre and goes all the way to infinity in both directions: to the Left and to the Right. The Infinity on the Left represents the concept of complete and universal equality among all humans, and the Infinity on the Right represents the opposite concept of ultimate inequality.

| Infinity | Left | | Right | Infinity |
|---|---|---|---|---|
| Communism | | Centre | Slavery | |

In real life, however, the extreme Left and the extreme Right are so similar that a model with a single infinity point seems to work better. Representing infinity with a point might appear somewhat counterintuitive. However, it can be easily rationalized if we apply a tiny bit of math. Although a circumference occupies a finite amount of space, the number of points on the circumference is infinite and is exactly the same as the number of points on a straight axis. Consequently, each point on the straight axis can be mapped to a specific point on the circumference and vice versa. Points farther from the Centre on one model map to points farther from the Centre on the other model. Thus the point representing infinity on the circular model becomes the convergence point; that is, you can come infinitely close to it but can never reach it. Essentially, the choice between these two models is somewhat similar to the ancient flat-Earth model versus the modern spheric Earth.

Although our circular model is two-dimensional, it's rather convenient to discuss it in terms of three-dimensional space. We can regard it as a cross section of a globe. This way we can take advantage of the geographical terminology, which very naturally lends itself to our discussion.

Imagine the equator line on a globe that is resting straight in front of us at the eye level. Focus on the equator line and disregard the rest of the globe. Then all we'll see at this angle will be a straight segment. The point in the middle, where the prime meridian crosses the equator, represents the political Centre. We'll also keep in mind that what we see is only one half of the model and that there is the second 180-degree arc that we cannot see from our position, because it's behind the horizon. The point antipodal to the Centre is the point where the date-line meridian crosses the equator; it can be called Infinity. It represents the imaginary point where there is no difference between the Left and the Right.

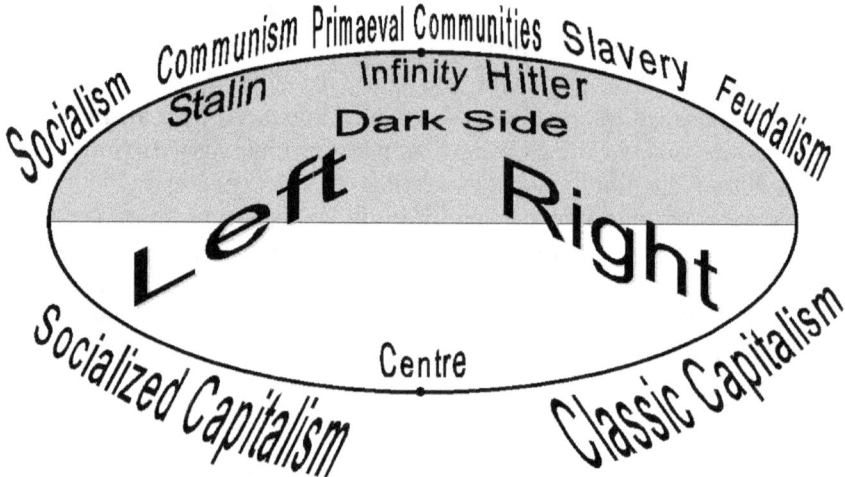

At the beginning of Time, we were somewhere around the Infinity point. There was no society in any meaningful sense of it; hence the concepts of Left and Right were then irrelevant. As we became more self-aware and developed the beginnings of social consciousness, we probably moved a little into the Left territory. Everyone was equal, but stronger and smarter individuals were probably a bit more equal than others. When that primaeval inequality transgressed into slavery, we crossed the Infinity point into the Right territory and started a journey from the Right to the Left via the Centre.

Historically, the Right have always been associated with inequality, the level and nature of it varying over time. Direct ownership of some humans by other humans being the ultimate form of inequality justifies our plotting slavery in the extreme-Right zone close to Infinity. Chronologically, slavery was followed by feudalism and then capitalism. Serfdom was one tick less oppressive than slavery, and then came capitalism, with all humans legally free and equal. Since the Lefts' officially proclaimed goal is human equality, it seems logical to define the progress from slavery to feudalism to capitalism as movement to the Left. Keep in mind though that our model represents the political spectrum, not the time line. This means that a specific point on the model corresponds to a specific level of equality (or inequality) among humans, not to a specific historic period or level of technological development. For example, if in the future we moved to an area somewhere in the vicinity of Infinity, it wouldn't mean that we'd travel back in time to the dawn of history or that we'd necessarily live in caves.

As capitalism has been evolving from its rudimentary forms into a welter of its modern-day shades and flavours, people's overall living standards have been rising and individual freedoms increasing. This means we finally emerged from behind the eastern horizon in our model and have been moving across the visible segment due west, towards the Centre. In 1917, Russia impatiently dashed to the Left, disappeared behind the western (i.e., left-hand-side) horizon, and was soon followed by a bunch of smaller countries from eastern Europe. On the opposite side, in the 1930s, Hitler dragged Germany so far back to the Right, to the Dark Side, that he and Stalin could clearly see each other across the Infinity point. Epochal as those two phenomena were, they were still only minor perturbations in the big scheme of things. Hitler suffered a crushing defeat at the hands of his nemeses, and Russia returned into the fold on its own. So, presently, we are all clustered mostly in the visible half of the model, somewhere around the Centre, some countries a bit to the Right of it and some a bit to the Left. Generally speaking, we, humanity as the whole, could proceed from here in either direction, but as the life would have it, we are now sliding to the Left.

The *why* part—why this is happening—is sufficiently clear. One of the Lefts' most notable strengths is their rhetoric, which is exceedingly attractive to brains either unsophisticated (like those of some youngsters who honestly believe they somehow know it all) or too busy or simply lazy to give anything a second thought. Equality, especially if properly garnished and served on a beautiful plate, almost always gathers more followers than "the fittest should win" paradigm. The latter makes a lot more sense from the logical standpoint if our ultimate goal is survival of humanity. However, a great majority of us subconsciously feel very insecure about themselves and are afraid of not coming out as winners in a natural-selection-based world. Consequently, it often takes great courage to overcome this psychological threshold and force oneself to think logically rather than emotionally.

What remains moot is the *where* part—where exactly we are going. If we keep heading to the Left, how far are we prepared to go? Are we going to stay in the visible part of our model, perhaps where western Europe is now hovering, or are we going to disappear behind the western horizon to the spot previously occupied by the Soviet Union? Or might we even keep going all the way to Infinity?

To answer these questions, we should take a closer look at the Lefts' internal makeup. The Left comprise two main categories; we'll call them the *evil* and the *misguided*. Terminology is up to us, remember? We can call them anything we want, as long as we clearly define what is what. To be fair, we should admit that evil transcends political lines; the Right have more than enough of this category among them too. But that's beside the point because we are discussing the Left at the moment.

The *evil* Left know exactly what they are doing. What they want is power—for the sake of the power itself. For them, power is not a means to an end; the goal of power is power. They are not trying to ascend into power to make our lives better; they are pretending to be trying to make our lives better so that we would vote them into power.

The *misguided* Left honestly believe they know better what's good for us, better than we do ourselves. Thus they, too, need power—to drag us, even to force if necessary, to their version of a politically correct happy life—for our own good, of course.

There are also all sorts of strands, factions, and subcategories, but as we are trying to focus on the big picture, we can safely disregard them. Although they are extremely noisy and some are often violent, overall they are not as dangerous as they might appear. They are just "useful idiots" for the *evil*. The exact origin of this term is moot; supposedly it was first used to refer to the people who lived in the Free World and supported—openly or covertly—the Stalinist Soviet Union. They were under the illusion that they were friends of the Soviet Union, whose leadership, in fact, scoffed at them. Clearly, those "useful idiots" are part of the *misguided* category. For example, there is a number of mostly young people who know and understand almost nothing about the real-life communist regimes and who openly proclaim communism as their goal. They have been overdosed with the Marxist propaganda generously administered to them by the *evil* category.

The bulk of the *misguided* believe that their goal is to smoothen the negative effects of the most blatant inequalities of capitalism and then to stop and live happily ever after somewhere to the left of the Centre, maybe about half-way to the western horizon, just about where western European countries are now. We've already briefly discussed some of the niceties of that spot. So, the question now is not whether that place is good or bad, but rather whether we'll be able to *stop* there.

As our recent history has clearly demonstrated, the socialist/communist models don't work. No matter how much popular support the Left had been able to rally at the beginning, eventually—if they managed to stay in power long enough—they had to start slaughtering or sending to "re-education" camps those same people whose lives they originally "intended" to improve. Why didn't it ever work? Lots of factors must have played their part in those failures. Some of them we discussed in the previous chapters, but except perhaps a few history scholars, no one knows the exact answer, and unfortunately, not too many people even seem to care much about it.

The nature of the *evil* category is not unique to the Left. Rather, its roots lie in the darkest corners of the human mind in general. Some people have an insatiable craving for power. Maybe there is a gene lurking somewhere deep down in our DNA that once helped early humans to survive in a hostile primaeval environment. We'll leave those details for biologists and psychiatrists to sort out. From the social perspective, the ultimate goal of the *evil* is to acquire unrestricted power over humankind and to hold on to it forever.

The *evil* Right are the big-time capitalists who are working to grow their businesses to the point where everything will belong to just a handful of individuals. Their strategy is to take over smaller businesses, one at a time, until there are no more of those left. The *evil* Left are advocates of socialism (they usually prefer to keep quiet about communism for the time being). They are working towards the same goal as their counterparts on the Right but via a different route. Under socialism, all means of production are to be nationalized and thus become property collectively owned by all the people. Sort of. The trick is that, for obvious logistical reasons, billions of people practically cannot collectively manage their vast holdings. Hence they'll have to delegate this function to a small number of their trusted representatives. And guess who will become those trusted ones? Although those reps will not, technically, own anything, being in charge of everything will have pretty much the same effect as if they did. The *evil* Right are by no means less evil, but for now we need not worry about them, because we are presently moving to the Left.

## 2084

Around 1948, a British writer commonly known to the world under the name of George Orwell wrote a novel titled *Nineteen Eighty-Four*. Some editions present the title in a numeric form, as *1984*. The novel describes a futuristic world divided among three gigantic empires. They were each practicing their own brands of socialism, which didn't differ much. Their common strategy was to limit consumption and keep their subjects in poverty as much as possible. The rationale behind this was that it was virtually impossible to control people in a society with high living standards, where a majority of population enjoyed most of what the civilization had to offer. Whereas in a society where never was enough food to eat and where people were constantly rummaging for even minor necessities like razor blades or shoe laces, a smallest handout could make all the difference in one's life.

Of course, controlling the economy alone wouldn't be enough to keep the starved and ripped off subjects in check forever. To perpetuate their stranglehold on the people, the rulers had to control everyone's minds, too. The omnipotent and omniscient Thought Police were tasked with ruthlessly and relentlessly eradicating any and all unorthodoxy, thus sealing the vicious cycle.

But that was a work of fiction, wasn't it? Such a horrible thing could never happen in real life, could it? No real human beings can be *that* evil, can they? ...

We'll move to the Left just a little bit more, just a few more tiny steps. And don't worry, we'll stop right there, well before we come anywhere close to the western horizon of your stupid model—

Yeah, right. And the ultimate-power-hungry *evil* Left will, of course, undoubtedly be just too happy to abandon their evil goals and stay quietly more than half-way from their cherished destination. Like Sirens, they will keep singing their sweet songs to lull everyone into complacency, and they'll keep us running, crawling, traipsing, dragging, inching, shambling, nudging—whatever works—to the Left until we reach a point of no return, when they'll have enough power to take the rest of the power without our help or consent.

Perhaps the world we'll end up in will not be precisely as described in *Nineteen Eighty-Four*, but there's nothing, so far, to indicate that 2084 will be significantly less Orwellian.

# EPILOGUE

On a brighter note, 1984 came and went and—thank God!—nothing that Orwell had predicted in his novel happened. But Orwell's book was not a prediction; rather, it was a warning to us to be vigilant. His choice of the exact year was just a literary technique. It's a work of fiction, after all; the author never meant his readers to get a calendar and start ticking off days remaining till a New Dark Age. By the same token, the society he described might never happen precisely as presented in the novel. Orwell seems to have used the Stalinist Soviet Union as a prototype and extrapolated it into an imaginary future, where the regime perfected itself to the level of sheer insanity.

Similarly, 2084 here does not represent an exact point in time when the world will turn black, and this book is not a scientific prediction. Hopefully, we'll never cross over to the Dark Side—neither through the Left route nor through the Right. But it's not enough to merely hope or pray. Without our careful steering, left on its own, there is a very good chance that the world *will* end up in a place close enough to "2084", whether we keep travelling through the Left zone or turn around and dive too far back to the Right.

But what can we, ordinary people, do to prevent that? We are just a herd of nobodies with only one vote each. And even if our candidates sometimes win, once we've sent them out to legislate and rule, we have very little control over what they end up doing on our behalf. Well, voting for the right candidates is, indeed, extremely important. And one vote each can tally up to millions. However, that is not the only thing we can do. How often do we talk to our kids, parents, siblings? How many times a year do we meet with our friends or stop to chat with our neighbours? What do we usually talk about? Weather? Work? Social gossip? That's OK; those are all legitimate topics. But we shouldn't shy away from politics either. It's not too hard to dedicate a few minutes of your casual chit-chat with friends and family to discussing the issues of Left and Right. Make up your mind, decide on which side you are, and try to convince your interlocutors that your logic is correct.

Times have changed since 1917; the Left can no longer pull off a violent "proletarian" revolution in any civilized country that matters. Their main weapons now are disguise, deceit, and sweet talk. They need our votes to be able to accomplish anything from their agenda. But once most of us have learned to see through their ploys, to make them out for what they really are, regardless of the colour of the hats they might be wearing at the moment, they'll be doomed. If we all start paying attention and spreading the word, we'll no longer be a statistical mass of nobodies. We'll become the driving force of History. *That's* what we are meant to be.

# ABOUT THE AUTHOR

V al Bakh was born and grew up in the former Soviet Union. Shortly after its collapse, he left the country and eventually ended up in Canada. Val Bakh's first novel, *In the Cold*, is now available from Amazon as an e-book and as a paperback. The novel presents a unique, insider's view of the last years of the Soviet Union right before its collapse.

Presently, Val Bakh works as a technical writer and an IT consultant. He is also gearing up for a sequel, where he plans to throw Dmitry Makhov, the main character of *In the Cold*, into the centre of a new, thrilling adventure. Please stay tuned.

To find out more about Val Bakh and his books, visit his blog at http://valbakh.com.

www.ingramcontent.com/pod-product-compliance
Lightning Source LLC
Chambersburg PA
CBHW070623290526
45790CB00002B/971